THE
CHELSEA
STORY

A taste of things to come – Charlie Cooke celebrates a League Cup goal against Leeds, while Jack Charlton ruminates.

THE CHELSEA STORY

John Moynihan

Foreword by Sebastian Coe

ARTHUR BARKER LIMITED   LONDON
A subsidiary of Weidenfeld (Publishers) Limited

'Reform Chelsea indeed! "Pensioners" no longer, Chelsea cannot forswear its whimsical past as easily as that. Let Arsenal and all those who have been bred in the Highbury stable defy success if they will, we prefer our Chelsea – dear scapegrace Chelsea – as it has always been, free to pursue the even tenor of its unpredictable way, staunch in the belief that waywardness has its part to play in the human comedy as well as reliability. ...' (from a 1930s match report by Don Davies – 'Old International', *Manchester Guardian* – killed in the 1958 Munich air crash).

Copyright © John Moynihan 1982

Published in Great Britain by
Arthur Barker Ltd
91 Clapham High Street
London SW4 7TA

ISBN 0 213 16823 5

Printed in Great Britain by
Butler & Tanner Ltd, Frome and London

Contents

Foreword by Sebastian Coe

As I was born in West London, geographical fate narrowed the field down to four. It could have been picturesque Craven Cottage, it could have been Loftus Road, intimately nestled in the shadows of the BBC and White City. At a push I suppose it could have been Brentford. On New Year's Day 1967 it was Arsenal at Stamford Bridge, and it has been Chelsea ever since.

By the time I had come to take my seat on the benches in the old West stand the Chelsea odyssey had already been struck. Following the club could be as frustrating as chasing spilt mercury across a laboratory table.

In the few short years since I replaced objectivity with blind passion, the Blues have made three Wembley appearances, losing the first and third, but making history by winning the first replayed FA Cup Final. Relegation in 1975 seemed to be the end of the world, but Chelsea recovered and returned to the first division in 1977, only to be relegated again one year later. Mere statistics, however, can tell only a part of the story.

If sport is supposed to mirror society, and football sometimes to lead its trends, then Chelsea is a veritable social history spanning Edwardian refinement and King's Road decadence. The birth and early history of the club, no less chequered than the recent vagaries of Stamford Bridge, have been lovingly charted by John Moynihan in *The Chelsea Story*.

This is the story of triumph against the odds, of disappointment, of glorious cup-ties, of Wembley finals and of manic supporters – but never of lost causes.

Chelsea has instilled in its followers a sense of the glorious unpredictability of football, the humour and cruelty, that can both excite and devastate in ninety minutes. For those who can come to terms with this, and see it for what it is, may also take in their stride the mundane assignments of the everyday.

Sebastian Coe   *May 1982*

Acknowledgements

The following books have proved invaluable in researching *The Chelsea Story*:
Behind the Scenes in Big Football, by Leslie Knighton (Stanley Paul, 1947)
Chelsea, by Reg Groves (Newsservice Ltd, 1946)
Chelsea Champions – Fifty Years of Chelsea Football, by Albert Sewell (Phoenix, 1955)
Don Davies, An Old International, by Jack Cox (Stanley Paul, 1900)
Football is my Business, by Tommy Lawton, ed. Roy Peskett (Sporting Handbooks, 1946)
The Footballer's Companion, ed. Brian Glanville (Eyre and Spottiswoode, 1900)
Tommy Docherty Speaks, by Tommy Docherty (Pelham, 1967)
The Chelsea Football Book, ed. Albert Sewell (Stanley Paul, 1970–74).
This One's on Me, by Jimmy Greaves (Arthur Barker, 1979).

The author would like to thank the following for their equally invaluable assistance in the making of this book: Geoffrey Green, Alan Hoby, Bernard Joy, Jack Rollin, Philip Evans, Alex Granditsch, Frank Keating, and many colleagues from the Football Writers Association. Also – for the kind loan of photographs – Albert Sewell, Judith Albrow, Eamonn McCabe (*Observer*), Phil Sheldon (*Sunday Telegraph*) and George Hilsdon Jr; and Nicholas Garland for his cartoon on page 126.

The photographs in this book are reproduced by kind permission of the following: Judith Albrow: page 145 (below); Monte Fresco: 143; Hugh Hastings: vi, rear endpaper; George Hilsdon Jr: 16 (below); Charles Knight: 174; Eamonn McCabe: 152, 169; Phil Sheldon: 156, 158, 166, 167, 171. The remainder were supplied by the author.

Preface

There was no really logical reason why I should have become an ardent supporter of enigmatic, lovable Chelsea Football Club. Perhaps it was hearing a window cleaner murmuring the odd ode to Tommy Lawton and the Pensioners at my parents' house along the Fulham Road shortly after the end of the Second World War which did the trick – the Moscow Dynamos had been in town, and Ivan captured the imagination of a sporting public undernourished on a diet of powdered eggs and dried milk.

What the window cleaner said seemed to stir a sinew or two in someone otherwise not very concerned about muddy ball games. At any rate, a visit to Stamford Bridge in the austere autumn of 1946, when Manchester United came bustling out of the bomb sites to beat Chelsea, turned the Stamford Bridge club into a grand, irrevocable obsession for one schoolboy, at least. Movie stars, and American heroes in general at once gave way to the blue Brylcreemed giants who had performed on that damp night at the Bridge.

No wonder my family scratched their heads – why all the hanging about outside Stamford Bridge, the loss of appetite on match days, the horrible let-downs year after year, afternoon after afternoon? Haunting nightmares when Chelsea almost reached Wembley in 1950, only to be knocked out by a freak goal by Arsenal's Freddie Cox – we were like all young losing semi-final fans then, walking down Tottenham High Road kicking miserably at newspapers and cartons.

Chelsea, for many years, were like a beautiful but unforthcoming woman relentlessly pursued – producing disappointments was in their nature. They exasperated, they reached semi-finals, only to wave away the chance of reaching Wembley; they had the services of great goal-scorers like Tommy Lawton and Jimmy Greaves, but like Bernard Shaw's theory about the English and the prize galleries, they did not know what to do with them when they had them.

When Chelsea at last started winning things, old masochists down at the Bridge could hardly believe the Music Hall image had been banished, at least temporarily. They had loved the club for the fun and laughter, the turnabouts, the games that Chelsea would play brilliantly and yet lose 5-6 to Manchester United, comic nights when the floodlights failed at Stamford Bridge, thunder storms when Tom Finney swam along the wing to put the ball in the Chelsea net, golden afternoons when Greaves turned Billy Wright into a bent piece of liquorice, Wagnerian nights when Eddie McCreadie slid down the middle, slid past Gordon Banks, and scored.

Whatever their faults, and a catalogue of disagreeable upheavals following the opening of their new, almost ruinous stand, Chelsea, with their geographical position so close to Piccadilly, which inspired Henry Augustus Mears to found the club in 1905, with their facilities, traditions and cavalcades of ups and downs, are and have been an essential part of the English football scene. From this particular fan, and biographer, whose heart has not been entirely hardened by too much viewing from the Press box, a warm vote of thanks must go to all Chelsea footballers from the early days, but particularly warriors of more recent times. To name an eminent few: Johnny Harris, Tommy Lawton, Ken Armstrong, Roy Bentley, Frank Blunstone, Jimmy Greaves, Peter Bonetti, Charlie Cooke and Dave Webb, who really did score Chelsea's only winning goal in a FA Cup Final. And last but not least, Albert Sewell, pioneer of Chelsea's (and the country's) first magazine programme in 1948, whose advice was invaluable in researching this book.

1

Fred Parker's Lucky Bite

Modern professional football was slow in coming to the heart of Britain's empire, the centre of the universe, Queen Victoria's proud capital, London Town. The roots of the game had been planted securely in the industrial north, the midlands, the north-east, and by those masters of dribbling, the Scots, in cities like Glasgow, Manchester, Nottingham, Newcastle and Birmingham, where writers of the period marvelled at the lure of the round ball.

One of them could hardly contain his pen in describing a match in Manchester 'which caused football fever to rage. I never saw such unbounded enthusiasm in the city. Starting at Cromwell's monument, there was a continuous stream of vehicles right away to Hyde Road and pedestrians in similar processions. Five in a hansom cab was not an uncommon sight.'

Central London, at the start of the twentieth century, had frequent hansom cab traffic jams, though they were rarely caused by the regular enticement of what was fast becoming a national game. There were no Highburys, no White Hart Lanes, to provide football for the residents of a capital depressed by following the fortunes of an increasingly costly Boer War. True, FA Cup finals of the time attracted flat-capped and bowler-hatted crowds of a hundred thousand to the old Crystal Palace ground, but London was still far behind the provinces in building glamour football stadiums. This would be duly noted by an astute businessman named Henry Augustus Mears, and his sporting brother, J. T. Mears, who spied the potentiality of staging professional football at an old athletics stadium at Stamford Bridge, near the northern boundaries of Chelsea. The idea took a few years to become a realistic project – but once the process was in motion, the speed with which the professional team became Chelsea and emerged as a brash new boy among the suspicious occupants of the Football League's Second Division, must have amazed even those two pioneers, normally noted for their icy calm under big business pressures.

The area where the new club in 1905 set off on a first season that would lead to seventy years of fun, fame, frustration, maddening inconsistency and, at times, sheer hilarity for legions of masochists in support, was the opposite of the industrial bricked grime where soccer clubs flourished in the North. Chelsea, although a growing residential area, was still something of a village, populated by actors and artists and prosperous legal men, who, as one resident wrote, 'like to cultivate mutual acquaintance and support local interests'. This cheery social cosiness hardly welcomed the inclusion of a professional soccer team on its boundaries – or a sport played essentially by working men, and bullet-headed players chewing 'baccy'.

Chelsea, of course, was famous for the Royal Hospital – and its resident Pensioners – founded by Charles II, the Old Church built by Sir Thomas More, and its Bun House, a fashionable place to visit in the eighteenth century. Less organized ball games had been played on the Chelsea common, which was built over by property developers who, in the voracious manner of today, outlawed nature in pursuit of gain. Chelsea Common dwindled from forty acres to a small plot. The residential invasion saw the population in Restoration times increased along the environs of the King's Road and the River Thames from three hundred to about twelve thousand at the start of the nineteenth century. A mushroomed 1981 population census included the Prime Minister, Mrs Thatcher. But overall, Chelsea has generally been noted for its Bohemians rather than its resident politicians.

The foundation of the Chelsea Arts Club in 1891 created a headquarters for painters, with Whistler, creator of Thameside 'Nocturnes', its most famous founder-member. Turner had also lived in the borough, not to mention a succession of famous writers going back to Pepys, Swift, Steele and Addison, and in Victorian times, Ruskin, Swinburne, and the gregarious Oscar Wilde, who wrote his best-known play, *The Importance of Being Earnest*, at his home in Tite Street. Mark Twain was another famous resident – Chelsea certainly thrived through its artistic membership – but as for a football team! For that there was little enthusiasm, that is, until the Mears brothers began chatting in a public house about the challenge ahead.

As with all business projects, there were barriers to escalate before the product was launched. H.A. Mears, or 'Gus', as he was known by his friends, bought the lease of Stamford Bridge Athletic Ground in 1904 from its previous owners, the London Athletic Club. The Stamford Bridge site, bordered by the Fulham Road, had originally been used as a market garden, alongside which ran a railway line built on the bed of a Thames tributary. Nearby was the old Lillie Bridge stadium which had played host to the second FA Cup Final in 1873. Gus Mears wanted to turn the ground into a football stadium – but, ironically, almost changed his mind when he received a juicy offer from the Great Western Railway, intent on turning the site into a pedestrian coal-yard.

The meeting Mears had with Fred Parker, a close chum and financial whizzkid, to discuss the offer turned out to be extremely painful for Parker, but happily earned a budding new football club a stay of immediate execution. After listening to his friend's optimistic conclusions about Chelsea's 'fair' future, and the possibilities of renting out Stamford Bridge for Cup finals, Mears frowned, a maddening frown, which made Parker's optimism shoot down into the bottom of his well polished shoes.

No, Mears said, he wasn't at all convinced by Parker's financial figures – despite his own and his brother's, enthusiasm to own a football ground, the Great Western Railway offer was too handsome to turn down. That, as far as the future of an unknown football team was concerned seemed to be that. Chelsea might never have come into being as a lovable soccer team, but for the sudden and ferocious arrival of Mears's prize hound, as the two men were walking out of Stamford Bridge – probably for the last time. Parker let out a howl of pain as his friend's dog drove his teeth into a fleshy, slightly hairy leg.

'Your damned dog has bitten me,' the unfortunate Parker bellowed, hardly in keeping with that patriotic calm Edwardian yeoman were supposed to observe in those glorious days of the Empire.

'Damned Scotch terrier, always bites before he speaks,' Mears said.

Despite his gashed leg, the victim had to see the funny side of the joke. 'You are the coolest fellow I have ever met,' he replied. Then he received a shock answer, which was to alter London football club history – and bring the author to his typewriter seventy-eight years later.

'You took that bite well, Fred', Mears said, stopping in his tracks. 'Most men would have kicked up hell about it. Look here – I'll stand on your judgement about Stamford Bridge. Go to the chemist and get the leg seen to, and meet me here at nine tomorrow. Then we'll get busy.' Thanks to Parker's fortuitous bite, Chelsea Football Club was about to be born. It was not the last time a dog was to figure prominently in the life of a member of the Mears family. In 1966, a dog called Pickles rescued the Football Association from deep embarrassment by sniffing out the World Cup which had recently been stolen. The chairman of the FA at that time was Chelsea chairman Joe Mears, Gus's nephew.

After his momentous change of mind, Gus Mears wasted no time in checking out favourable designs for a new stadium. A spruce, square-shouldered, solidly built man with a bushy moustache – he was the opposite of the odd, scruffy, run-down artist on the breadline, whom he would pass while briskly walking down the Fulham Road. His persuasive powers must have impressed the Scottish architect Archibald Leitch, when they conferred over a porridge and haddock breakfast in a Glasgow hotel, where the budding Chelsea patron had taken the victim of his dog's bite. Mears and Parker were shown the great modern football stadiums of the time by Leitch – Hampden Park, Celtic Park and Ibrox Park – and from these inspections, the design of a brand new London football stadium was put to paper.

At first, Mears had ideas of renting out the stadium – which by the second month of 1905 was well on the way to construction – but an offer to Fulham FC to rent the stadium for the sum of £1,000 per annum was rebuffed. So a new club, capable of playing top-class football, was formalized, with Mears drawing up a list of backroom boys and general figureheads, before actually going out to buy a team. William Claude Kirby was named as chairman, a position he held until his death in 1935, and Lord Cadogan as president. The earl's light blue racing colours were originally chosen for the new club, but were changed later to the current royal blue.

The club's name, Chelsea, came into being only after long discussion – originally Mears and his team considered such names as London, Kensington and Stamford Bridge – and Chelsea took a long time to get the thumbs-up.

Henry Augustus Mears, founder of Chelsea Football Club.

There were no Third or Fourth Divisions in the Football League in those days – so Chelsea approached the Southern League for membership. No joy here, but this cold shoulder led to far better things. With the Stamford Bridge stadium coming along nicely, the huge slug of terracing on the far side built up with clay dug from the constructed Piccadilly Line, and partly with cinders from a local sewer, Mears – by now a Chelsea director and overall patron – and Parker, financial secretary, set their sights high. Having chosen the first Chelsea player-manager, John Tait Robertson, a Glasgow Rangers player, known to his Ibrox fans as Jackie, and the owner of sixteen Scottish caps, they launched into the transfer market in the spring of 1905 with a vigour in keeping with their hopes to make the club a flourishing concern in the Football League, where a vacancy existed in the Second Division.

A number of signings were made on the condition that Chelsea were elected, including Bob McRoberts from Small Heath (now Birmingham FC) for £100, and Jimmie Robertson, a promising inside-forward from the same club, for fifty pounds. Another transaction between Chelsea and Small Heath changed the career of a young inside-forward called Jimmy Windridge, a shy, charming young man but unheard of in the big-time. He cost Chelsea a modest £190 – not bad going considering that he played for England two seasons later – and was nicknamed 'Windridge the Wizard'.

Other signings included the world's fattest goalkeeper from Sheffield United, Willie Foulke, who stood 6 ft 3 in and weighed over twenty stone, and whose appetite matched his colossal hunger for the game, and who scared the life out of opposing forwards. The enormity of Foulke alone warranted inclusion in the persuasive promotional dossier the bowler-hatted Kirby and Parker presented when they attended the annual meeting of the Football League.

Let us consider the atmosphere, at the Tavistock Hotel in Covent Garden, on 29 May 1905. The League, being essentially Northern and Midland in membership, was represented by bluff men puffing pipes over their chain watches, making 'a spade is a spade' talk to the rattling sound of background brass. Rounds of Scotch and ale were liberally distributed to the members while new, potential members hung about on the side-lines, hoping for the votes to swing their way. Apparently as the meeting went on and on, Kirby, charging backwards and forwards by hansom to his office, and manager Robertson were by no means optimistic about

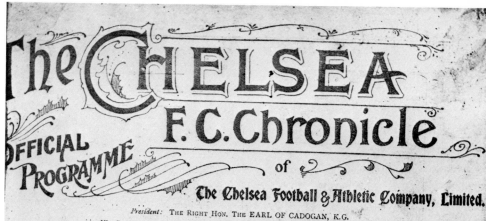

The CHELSEA F.C. Chronicle

OFFICIAL PROGRAMME

of The Chelsea Football & Athletic Company, Limited.

President: THE RIGHT HON. THE EARL OF CADOGAN, K.G.

Vice Presidents:
C. A. WHITMORE, ESQ., M.P.
COLONEL LESLIE POWELL, J.P.
C. B. FRY, ESQ.

W. HAYES FISHER, ESQ., M.P.
MAJOR W. F. WOODS, J.P.
H. VENN, ESQ.

Directors:
W. CLAUDE KIRBY, ESQ., *Chairman.*
H. A. MEARS, ESQ.   J. T. MEARS, ESQ.
A. F. JANES, ESQ.   H. BOYER, ESQ.
G. THOMAS, ESQ.   T. L. KINTON, ESQ.

Manager: MR. JOHN T. ROBERTSON.

Hon. Financial Sec. F. W. PARKER, ESQ.

Secretary: MR. WILLIAM LEWIS.

Colors: Light Blue and White.

Vol. i. No. 1.]   MONDAY, SEPTEMBER 4TH, 1905.   [One Penny.

DAISY CUTTERS.

"THEY'RE OFF!"

Racing men talk of "the saddling bell at Lincoln" in March.

Bah! It's at the "bottom of the League" compared with the first trill of the Ref's whistle in September.

Well, now what do you think of our Ground—and the stand—and the terracing? Good enough for SECOND Division Football, is it not?

And it is only a baby as yet. Wait until it is full grown, and then—well, we shall see what we Chel-sea.

Don't be over sanguine and expect *too* much of the teams at the first start. We don't expect to "stroll" into the First Division, but we *shall* get there in time.

One thing, we have a team of genuine triers, who are on the best of terms with themselves and with one another. If they cannot always command success, they will do their level best to deserve it.

Hearty congratulations to our friendly opponents to-day upon their elevation to the "Upper House."

And may we follow in their footsteps!

True, "We've got a long way to go," but we are good stayers, and one of our mottoes is "Excelsior."

Yes, that is one of our mottoes. We have another one, which we owe to (and is typical of) the Father of the Chelsea F.C.—Mr. "Gus" Mears. It is "Don't Worry."

When the baby-Club, a fine healthy child from the first, was scarcely opening its eyes upon the world, it found—like all good children in the fairy tales—an evil genius, which took the form of a Dakoit, seeking an opportunity to destroy it. Good word, Dakoit, look it up in Nuttall's. We had some anxious moments, but the "happy father" merely smiled good humouredly and said "Don't Worry!"

Then we had some more anxious moments. There were many and vexatious delays caused by various formalities with the constructional work, and doubts were freely expressed as to the completion of the Stands, &c., in time for the season. Again the same cheery optimism and emphatic "Don't Worry!"

And so the expression has become our watchword, and you will hear it twenty times a day at Stamford Bridge.

Bye-the-way, one of our most enthusiastic followers is "Count" Schomberg, who states that we "count" on him to follow the first team where they go. We cannot have too many of such sportsmen!

Chelsea's chances, but Parker, a wizard with a spy-glass when it came to spotting a breakthrough, bet the other pair five shillings cash that Chelsea would be elected. It was Parker who spoke up for Chelsea, a task made the more difficult by the inability of some delegates to keep their eyes open – the music halls and beer parlours had done good business the night before. Parker weighed in with his account of the bright new world of Stamford Bridge – (A) Financial stability (Chelsea already had three thousand pounds in the bank); (B) a super new stadium in keeping with a First Division team; (C) a potentially strong football team, blessed with many sound signings.

Now came the crunch. The delegates, having heard Parker's three-minute speech, were ready to vote – and Parker, his small moustache twitching nervously, released a final entreaty to the assembly: 'I will not trespass on you further beyond suggesting that when you consider the points I have put before you, you will come to the conclusion that you cannot refuse us.'

It was an Edwardian aria as robust and enticing as anything sung that evening at the nearby Royal Opera House. Chelsea were elected on the first ballot to the Second Division.

2

'Have You Seen Little Willie?'

Once Fred Parker's succinct promotional oration had succeeded, the task at hand was to get eleven strapping footballers on to the field for Chelsea's first season in League combat. When Parker, chairman Kirby and the rest of the early backroom pioneers held a celebration, Gus Mears, who would retain overall control of the club until just before the First World War, raised a warning finger: 'Well, that's that,' he said, looking out at a new Stamford Bridge stadium rapidly nearing completion. 'Now for the struggle. I suppose the first five years will be the worst.' There was a touch of irony about that remark, for while Chelsea gained promotion to the First Division two years after their birth, some of the really 'worst' times in Stamford Bridge history came much later in the 1970s and early 1980s. Prophesies can sometimes lie dormant, full of malice like rusty but lethal mines below the surface.

Now the scene shifted from boardroom tactics to the sweaty Edwardian emphasis on pre-season training, with player-manager John Tait Robertson getting the lads out on the road to work off excess tummies. Some of the squad had already seen the world's fattest goalkeeper before, some hadn't, and the majority had certainly not seen Bill Foulke in his birthday suit swaggering around, 6 ft 3 in tall and over twenty-two stones.

'My word,' whispered Parker, the financial wizard, as Foulke menacingly bore down on him. 'Darkness covers the earth.' With his ill-fitting suit, small cap popped on top of a shaven, bullet head, Foulke stalked rather than walked, carrying his bulbous belly proudly like an ostrich with a prize egg. The mere whiff of food would send him trailing around the environs of the Fulham Road in search of ten bangers to demolish. In eating terms alone, he was the world's champion custodian.

Foulke had taken up his appointment as Chelsea's first goalie – a position occupied in later decades by many fine keepers, including Howard Baker, Vic Woodley, and Peter Bonetti – with a formidable reputation for deeds both on and off the field. Nowadays, John Tait Robertson might have quivered when told of Foulke's less than engaging qualities – but, when a bit of letting off steam was regarded as part of football's charm, the Chelsea manager let the big bully get on with it. Foulke was not over-fond of forwards, including his own, and he hated referees. Rival forwards were to be picked up and held in front of two piercing eyes; referees were to be abused, scolded and sworn at before, during and after matches.

Foulke, a native of Wellington, Shropshire, had made his name with Sheffield United, winning recognition for England, and two Cup Winners medals in three Final appearances between 1899 and 1902. Ancient newsreel clips show him in action in goal at Crystal Palace, his ballet tights bulging with fat as the big man charged menacingly at opposing forwards, fists clenched, his jaw solid. The giant was not without humour – when he came to Chelsea at the age of twenty-nine, he insisted on taking the field alongside the smallest player in the team, Martin Moran. This raised regular hoots of laughter from the Chelsea Music Hall following, and earned Foulke the nickname 'Little Willie'.

His appetite was prodigious – and it is said that on one occasion his Chelsea team-mates came down for dinner on an away trip to find the custodian had demolished the lot: 'I don't care what they call me as long as they don't cali me late for dinner,' he quipped. As for referees, the memory of Foulke's bulbous shadow sent them scampering for pen and journal. J.T. Howcroft, of Bolton, was one of them, victim of Foulke's excesses during a match between Burslem and Chelsea. 'The giant goal-keeper must have got out of bed on the wrong side, as he seemed to have a grouse against more than one opponent. Ultimately, when a Burslem player made for goal, Foulke did not bother about the ball but grabbed the player round the middle and hurled him into the back of the net. I pointed at once for a penalty kick. Then the fun started. It took quite a time to persuade Foulke to get into his proper position and it seemed to me he was after my scalp.

'Eventually J.T. Robertson, Chelsea's captain, took the bull by the horns and told Foulke to go into goal or clear out. He did not try and save the shot but stood glaring at me. I kept a respectable distance until the end of the game, and then made my way faster than usual to the dressing-room. If Foulke had put one of those large hands on me I might have been short of some of my anatomy.'

Howcroft, by coincidence, had run the line in the 1902 Cup Final when Sheffield United lost to Spurs after a replay – and Foulke plainly kept the Bolton official's name firmly in his well-stocked book of people to be nasty to on future meetings. It was in the first match against Spurs at Crystal Palace that Foulke reacted in a way that probably would have earned him a *sine die* ban in later generations. At the end of the match Foulke menaced the referee, Tom Kirkham, because he thought a goal against him had been offside. Kirkham waddled off to the dressing-room and locked himself in. It was Frederick Wall, the FA secretary, who eventually came to the rescue, persuading a naked Foulke that tearing down the door of the referee's dressing-room with his bare hands would land him in the brig. Mr Kirkham recalled: 'The thing I can never forget is Foulke, 6 ft 3 in tall, and tremendous in size, striding along the corridor without a stitch of clothing.'

Sartorially, Foulke was a bit of a dandy and used to frequent clothiers' shops along the Fulham and Kings Roads in Chelsea long before the era of Swinging London, gaudy T shirts, the Stones and Mary Quant. His favourite shopping area was Walham Green (now Fulham Broadway), where the counter-assistants nicknamed the fat man 'baby' – his collar size was twenty-four, and he needed constant replacements to provide starchy cover for a steamy, bull-like neck. In winter, he liked sporting a silk scarf, with a gold pin attached to show he was king custodian.

I suppose Foulke in these more slim-line and weight conscious times would now be regarded as something of a circus freak, but his fatness disguised remarkable agility for such a large man. He could punch a football, one of the old soggy, hog-skin variety, beyond the half-way line; high centres he easily snatched away from threatening rivals; and he could get down too with a tumbling agility even a wiry Charlie Chaplin could not match in his impression of Sniffy the Goalkeeper at Chelsea Palace. And Foulke was a master at saving penalties – he literally filled the goal, and opponents found the greatest difficulty in squeezing the ball past the giant. One Burton United player complained that there was no room on either side of Foulke to shoot.

John Tait Robertson, Chelsea's first manager, 1905.

MCROBERTS. KEY. WINDRIDGE. MACKIE. FOULKE (captain). COPELAND. J. T. ROBERTSON. MCEWAN. MORAN. KIRWAN

Chelsea's original team, 1905–06. The elephantine figure in the middle is Willie Foulke.

A side-on view of Foulke filling the goal-mouth.

Action at Stamford Bridge during the first season – 1905–06.

Foulke kept goal for Chelsea when they played their first Second Division match away to Stockport County on 2 September 1905 – a game Chelsea were to lose by 1–0 in front of only six thousand spectators. In those less cushioned days for professional footballers, players and manager had to tramp from the station to the stadium at away matches, often an uphill trudge through dingy districts. As usual, Foulke stalked menacingly through the town for Chelsea's introduction to League football, until suddenly drawing up in alarm like an elephant sensing danger. A Stockport nipper had pulled him by the trouser leg and cried: 'Eee, you'll get whacked t'day.'

'Then it will be for the first time for Chelsea, m'lad.'

Foulke turned out for the Pensioners (as Chelsea were quickly nick-named) at Stamford Bridge the following Wednesday, when the Fulham Road fans had their first sight of the giant in action – 'gads' and 'gollies' wafted towards the roof of the new stand as Foulke trundled menacingly along his goal-line – but it was the gifted Jimmy Windridge who enter-tained the crowd, scoring the new club's first hat-trick in the 5–1 defeat of Hull City. Chelsea finished a respectable third that season, behind Bristol City and Manchester United. It was United who drew the first sixty thousand crowd to Stamford Bridge, as they were to do regularly in later years, when Matt Busby's legions dropped in. In the FA Cup, Gus Mears's 'babies' lost 7–1 in the third round to Crystal Palace – but the club had put out a reserve team because of an important League match the same day. This brought in a new FA rule making full strength teams in Cup matches compulsory under threat of heavy fines.

After that first season, Foulke moved to Bradford City, where he finished his official footballing career. The rest of the Chelsea dressing-room may have welcomed the extra freedom allowed for more puny rib cages after his departure – but there was less excuse for laughs and jokes about the everyday adventures surrounding the big man and his belly. Foulke's last days before he died from an insolent chill in 1916 were spent on Blackpool Sands earning coins from volunteers in a 'beat Little Willie' penalty-kick challenge. A sad, untidy ending for one of the great charac-ters of the game.

Chelsea's second season was altogether successful, as second place and promotion were gained with a total of fifty-seven points. It also marked the arrival in the first team of another great character – Chelsea's history is crowded with them – but this, unlike Foulke, was a demon, hard-hitting centre-forward. His name was George Hilsdon, signed by John Tait Robertson after the shrewd Scot saw him playing for West Ham reserves. Hilsdon, a nineteen-year-old no-nonsense thruster, scored five goals in his first Chelsea match on 1 September 1906 against Glossop. That 9–2 result is still Chelsea's record League score. Hilsdon finished the season with twenty-seven goals, eleven more than his talented colleague, Windridge. Hilsdon became something of a legend at Stamford Bridge, and the weather-vane on top of the old main stand was modelled on him. Some sooth-sayer claimed that when this was taken down, as it was when the stand was pulled down in the 1970s, Chelsea would have a long run of misfortune. And so it proved.

'Gatling-Gun' Hilsdon, as the East Ender was affectionately nicknamed by the Chelsea fans, continued to rat-tat-tat goals for the Pensioners in their new position of eminence – in a Cup match against Worksop, Chelsea won 9–1, Hilsdon scoring six of them. It was the type of scoring that even eluded Jimmy Greaves in his Chelsea heyday. Hilsdon was hero of the Fulham Road. His son, George Hilsdon Jr., now seventy-six and still an eminent actor, remembers the awe in which the fans held his father as he strode along the pavement from Walham Green to Stamford Bridge:

'People followed father around the streets. He scored some fantastic goals for Chelsea, beating five men and putting the ball away. They called him the "Mushroom" centre-forward because he emerged on the scene in such a dramatic fashion, winning an England place soon after he joined the club, and there were some good centre-forwards around in those days – Harry Hampton and Alf "Blaze of Glory" Common to name two. One of father's assets was his strength of thigh; he was very hard to knock off the ball.'

Hilsdon's glamour contrasted with the overall impression that the club presented on the field – Chelsea often found it hard to survive in the improved status they had played for and won a place in. It was time to appoint a full-time manager, and David Calderhead, described as a 'kindly, sphinx-faced Scot', arrived to take over from Robertson. He had been a loyal servant to Leicester City, first as a centre-half at the end of Queen Victoria's reign, then as manager. Calderhead was to stay on at Chelsea until 1933 – a long time in office as boss of the Old Unpredictables.

Hilsdon remained at Chelsea for six seasons, blazing in goals from the

George Hilsdon, doyen of Chelsea's
Edwardian centre-forwards, wearing
England colours.

CHELSEA FOOTBALL CLUB, 1908-1909.

MOIR (Assist. Trainer), REILLY, CANE, CARTWRIGHT, CAMERON, KENNEDY, HARDING, H. RANSOM (Trainer),
MILLER, A. J. PALMER (Assist. Sec.), D. CALDERHEAD (Sec. Manager), HENDERSON, WARREN, ROBINSON, BRAWN, DOUGLAS, DOLBY, WHITLEY, BIRNIE, McKENZIE, KEY.
Directors—G. SCHOMBERG, J. H. MALTBY, H. A. MEARS, W. CLAUDE KIRBY (Chairman), J. T. MEARS, F. W. PARKER, T. L. KINTON, E. H. JANES.
WALTON, FREEMAN, ROUSE, HILSDON, McROBERTS (Captain), WINDRIDGE, HUMPHREYS, BRIDGEMAN, FAIRGRAY.

Dorrett & Martin.   [COPYRIGHT.]   16 Belle Vue Road,
                                                                     Upper Tooting, S.W.

The old Chelsea weather-vane. It was dismantled in 1972 when the stand was demolished, incurring the run of ill-luck which had been prophesied many years earlier. The figure was supposedly modelled on George 'Gatling-Gun' Hilsdon.

David Calderhead, Chelsea's manager for three decades.

edge of the box, and booting home penalties past cringing goalkeepers. The crowd on the wet and windy Stamford Bridge terraces loved him, but there was trouble afoot, as often happens when a star twinkles too brightly, and the con-men and hangers-on move in. Hilsdon had won England caps against Scotland, Wales and Northern Ireland in the Home Championship, and taken part in a pioneering England tour of Austria, Hungary and Belgium, at a time when the old country still lorded it over other nations. Despite his menial pay – four pounds a week – the club did try to make Hilsdon's standard of living a little more comfortable, Gus Mears personally handing his prize player a pound for every goal he scored. It was a time to celebrate, and like other leading Chelsea performers down the years, Hilsdon fancied a jar or two on the way home. He became a familiar figure in the Chelsea, Battersea and Fulham taverns – and there was always another drink available from a kindly soul toasting 'Our Gatling-Gun George'.

George Hilsdon Jr. puts his father's heavy imbibing into perspective: 'What wasn't widely known at the time was that my mother had chronic asthma. It affected her terribly – and affected father as well. He used to come home and see her suffering – it was not surprising that after a while he started taking a drink or two.' Hilsdon's form began to decline, he could no longer find the energy to pound through defences, and those one-pound goal bonuses from Gus Mears began to decrease. Eventually Chelsea sold him back to West Ham, for whom he turned out at inside-left in the 1912-13 season. But Hilsdon's best times had been west of Plaistow as Chelsea battled on, teased unmercifully by the music hall comedians, including one of the masters, George Robey. Robey himself once turned out for the Pensioners in a charity match, and signed amateur forms for them afterwards, which led to one appearance in the reserves and a goal miss from two yards out. 'I only joined Chelsea to keep them in the First Division,' the comic quipped.

As for Hilsdon, his own subsequent career was something akin to a Russian tragedy. 'Father was still an idol when he played for West Ham,' George junior remembers, 'but the First World War put an end to all that. He joined the East Surrey Regiment, but it was not until the last year of the war that he had to fight. A kindly brigadier had kept him out of the trenches, because he was the king of the regimental soccer and cricket teams, but then came the last big German push, and father copped the mustard gas at Arras.'

Hilsdon experienced excruciating pain in his legs from that foul, frothy poison – and he never played senior football again. A job as player-manager of a non-League club proved some consolation but, putting it bluntly, Hilsdon was on the skids. Running a pub proved a failure, and then followed a frustrating period making tea on building sites. When he died at Leicester in 1941 from tuberculosis, the Football Association paid for the funeral. It was war-time, and only four people, including his son, turned up. But quite a few veteran Chelsea supporters nodded their heads in sympathy when they heard the news. For many of them, George had been the best ever.

3

All Dressed up in Khaki

'Our men ... go steadily on to the German frontline. Brilliant sunshine and a haze of smoke drifting along the landscape. Some Yorkshires ... cheering as if at a football match. The sunlight flashes on bayonets ... Shrapnel bursting in small bluish white puffs with tiny flashes. The birds seem bewildered; a lark begins to go up and then flies feebly along, thinking better of it ... I am staring at a sunlit picture of Hell ...'

Siegfried Sassoon

For Lieutenant Vivian Woodward, a young English officer returning from the battlefields of France in the spring of 1915, a few days' leave from scenes such as described above by the distinguished English poet was a respite from the horrors of war.

But for Woodward, a tall, upstanding Essex man, whose neat civvy blazers revealed him as a spruce dresser raised as a youth in the more carefree Edwardian times, his leave pass to Blighty was a ticket to something rather more special. Woodward, a famous amateur footballer of his time, and an architect by profession, had promised to take a train up to Old Trafford, Manchester to watch his own team, Chelsea, play in their first Cup final. He had underlined, in a letter from France, that none of the lads who had taken Chelsea to their first final should be displaced.

In years preceding the War, Woodward, who had arrived at Stamford Bridge from Tottenham as an emergency gesture when the club had seventeen players on the injury list, formed a destructive partnership with Hilsdon and Windridge – an all-England inside trio. Woodward's ability to hold the ball and run long distances, despite the attentions of rustic defenders, marked him as one of the great players of his era. But international calls deprived Chelsea for long periods of their prized trio – and led to the club's relegation to the Second Division in 1910, with only eleven wins in thirty-eight games. It took them two years to return to the First Division, and it was Woodward's inspiration, and the arrival of a new battling centre-forward, Bob Whittingham, a war horse in the penalty-area, which helped do the trick.

Chelsea had just missed promotion in 1911 and reached the semi-final of the FA Cup, losing to Newcastle. Despite their increasing reputation for being music hall clowns, their inconsistency helping fan the titters of their audiences, and a number of acts of indiscipline by members of the playing staff tempted by two o'rums in the pubs of Fulham and Hammersmith, the club's popularity increased. In 1911 a crowd of 77,952 spectators came along to watch a fourth round cup-tie – a record Cup gate at that time – as Swindon were beaten 3-1 at Stamford Bridge, Whittingham scoring two of the goals.

Whittingham put thirty-two goals away for Chelsea in League games in the 1910-11 season, and thirty the following season when promotion was gained. Goalkeepers were anxious every time Whittingham forced his way through, driving in splendid goals from long distances. One remarked somewhat timorously: 'I would rather face his Satanic majesty than Whittingham.'

It was Woodward, however, famous for his sportsmanship, Corinthian manners and temperance – one Chelsea player had been suspended at the time for drunkenly knocking out a cab horse – who made Chelsea's return to the First Division a reality in the last game of the 1911-12 season. It was one of those tense occasions that were to feature several times in later Chelsea decades.

They had to beat Bradford Park Avenue at Stamford Bridge that late-April day to make sure of promotion, but Burnley were level with Chelsea in second place. If both Chelsea and Burnley won, then goal average would decide it. It was a cliff-hanger if ever there was one, and the subject of much conversation in the local taverns.

The Chelsea team that day is worth recording: Molyneux, loyal Jim, who kept goal for Chelsea for many seasons; Bettridge, described by Calderhead, the Chelsea manager, as 'the pluckiest little player that ever pulled on a football boot', and Cartwright; Taylor, Ormiston and Harrow, one of the most renowned full-backs to wear the Chelsea shirt; Douglas, Whittingham, Woodward, Freeman and Bridgeman.

A heavy League programme, which required Chelsea to play three games in a week, did the home team's stamina no favours, but a thirty thousand crowd, blowing hot enthusiasm beneath their cloth caps, got behind Chelsea and Whittingham laid on a first goal for Charlie Freeman in the thirty-second minute. It was to prove the only goal, but the promotion-winning one, because Burnley lost their match. Pandemonium

Mr Claude Kirby (*left*), Chelsea's first chairman, showing new manager Leslie Knighton round Stamford Bridge in 1933. Kirby died two years later.

Opposite:
Above A famous victory against a famous side. . . . Two years later they reached the FA Cup Final against Sheffield United. Vivian Woodward (*seated second from right*) was on leave from the trenches, but sportingly declined to play.

Below left Vivian Woodward.

Below right Jack Harrow.

The First CHELSEA Team To Beat ASTON VILLA. Oct 25th 1913

followed the final whistle, with fans invading the pitch and hugging their heroes. As for gentleman Vivian Jack Woodward, he was showered with congratulations as he left the ground. For Woodward, his call-up with the flower of England's youth was only two years away. But that night, with hostilities still a matter of speculation, and as the war lords of Europe rattled their sabres, Woodward raised a glass to his team, and said, 'Well done, chaps.'

In the two seasons prior to the First World War, Chelsea's return to the seniors was at first hesitant – in eighteenth place in 1913 they barely escaped relegation – and then moderately good: in 1914 they were eighth. But new players of talent were arriving to assist Vivian Woodward and his 'chaps': Nils Middelboe, an orderly wing-half from Denmark, whom old codgers at Stamford Bridge still talk about with affection today; Harold Halse, a Leyton boy, blessed with a clouting shot, and well known by Chelsea supporters for scoring three goals apiece in both halves for Manchester United in the first Charity Shield match at Stamford Bridge. Halse had won an FA Cup medal with Aston Villa in 1913 – glorious days for this talented inside-right, staring benevolently from behind a bushy moustache in team photographs. Halse teamed up with a one-eyed centre-forward called Bob Thomson, a burly man from Croydon, who surmounted his disability with cheerful Cockney wit. Interviewed once by a zealous scribe who wanted to know how anyone could possibly play with one eye, Thomson leaned against a lamp-post and reflected: 'When the ball is coming my way I shut the other eye and play from memory.'

By now the Great War was very much past the sabre-rattling stage, as battalions of volunteers marched through Chelsea and Fulham on their way to stations, barracks and basic training. The Football League pro-gramme went along uneasily, with more and more players leaving their clubs to go to France. One of the first to volunteer had been Woodward, an eager recruit to the Footballers' Battalion. His career at Chelsea was virtually at an end, although he survived the war and became a director of the club afterwards. It was at the front that Woodward heard at least one piece of good news – a good Cup run for the Blues.

In this last season of 1914–15, before League football was suspended until the end of the war, Chelsea contrived to reach their first Cup final. Woodward and his fellow troops turned away from ever-increasing columns of war news in their papers to note that Chelsea had beaten Swindon Town somewhat luckily following a replay in the first round.

Indeed, Chelsea were fortunate to get through, because the West Country team were leading by 2–1 with normal time running out. Then Harry Ford, who had been educated along the Kings Road, popped up to equalize. Chelsea went through in extra time by 5–2.

Woodward was equally delighted to read that Chelsea had survived the next round, beating Arsenal 1–0 with a Halse goal. The third round victims were Manchester City – again by a single goal. And while many Geordies in the trenches may not have thought it very funny, Stamford Bridge supporters in khaki let out a great mocking cheer at the news of their team's replay victory at St James's Park against Newcastle, pride of the Magpies. Again the hero was Ford, scoring the only goal. Then came the semi-final against Everton at Villa Park, and once again the news was good for Chelsea supporters in Flanders, and Woodward could not resist raising a mug of tea to hail a 2–0 victory, in which Jimmy Croal and Halse scored the goals.

Croal, a Falkirk schoolmaster, had been signed before the start of the season in company with Bob McNeil, a Hamilton Academicals outside-left. They had flourished as a left-wing pair for the Scottish League, and their arrival was the prelude to many transfers from north of the border to Stamford Bridge. Croal, who was on Chelsea's books until 1922 when he went to Fulham, and McNeil, a Stamford Bridge regular until 1929, were initially to earn Cockney raspberries for holding up Chelsea's attacking movements with their delicate dribbling, but once they settled into the faster pace of English football, they became solid favourites with Chelsea fans. In McNeil's case this was revealed only recently, when older Stamford Bridge supporters wrote to *The Sunday Telegraph*, following an article on Chelsea wingers, to enquire why the greatest of them all had not been mentioned.

At any rate, Chelsea were now in the Cup Final. The venue was Old Trafford, Manchester; the opposition, Sheffield United. It was through the railroad confusion of wartime England that Captain Woodward made his way to watch his team in action, arguing good-naturedly in a train packed with fellow troops about the outcome of the game. When Woodward arrived in Manchester, he was met by Chelsea directors up from London for the Cup; they came straight to the point in their hotel lounge. They were worried about Bob Thomson's recently dislocated arm. Would it stand up to a Cup Final? 'You must play, Woodward,' said one, earnestly offering a Gold Flake. 'We need you for the Final!'

But Woodward desisted: 'No thank you, sir, Bob Thomson played in the earlier rounds and deserves his place. I will watch from the stand.' The words of a true Corinthian; the one-eyed Thomson was in, declaring himself fit before the kick-off. It was a final which, in retrospect, significantly introduced khaki to the terraces, particularly from the massed Sheffield contingent, many of whom a year later would be filing off to the carnage of the Somme. The day itself was a stinker: dark, wet, clouded by an evil yellow mist. The crowd, predominantly in uniform, cheerfully sang *Tipperary*. The Chelsea line-up was Jim Molyneux; Walter Bettridge and Jack Harrow; Freddy Taylor, Tom Logan and Andy Walker; Harry Ford, Harold Halse, Bob Thomson, Jimmy Croal and Bobby McNeil. A fair team, but ultimately, deprived of Woodward's inspired leadership and willowy running, a losing one.

If the playing conditions were bad, so was the morale and attitude of the London side throughout most of the match. Mistakes were made constantly, and one by the worthy Harrow, and a fumble by Molyneux, allowed United their first goal through Simmons before half-time. And two more United goals by Fazackerley and Kitchen made victory certain for the Yorkshire team shortly before the end of a miserable afternoon for Stamford Bridge. 'We were bad enough for a League match,' a Chelsea player grumbled after United had received the Cup. Bad, yes, but then Thomson, despite Woodward's loyalty, should plainly not have played, his dislocated arm giving him trouble during his rare rampages down the middle, and another injury to Ford hardly helped Chelsea either.

At the end, as they lined up for their losers' medals, they heard Lord Derby raise a patriotic voice towards dark, satanic, overcast skies. Wizard stuff for the recruiting officers from the Secretary of State for War: 'You have played well with one another and against one another,' Lord Derby barked. 'Play with one another for England now.'

It was with this inspiring ovation, which more than one First World War general would have approved of, that the men of Chelsea dispersed for the duration. One at least, Harry Wilding, would win the Military Medal with the Grenadier Guards. For over three more years of blood-letting, Chelsea residents remained on the alert for the nocturnal arrival of German zeppelins. Modern war no longer spared civilians.

4

Big Signings
and Music Hall Jokes
1919—1939

'I was almost a stranger when I moved to London, and Chelsea Football Club. I had never been too happy about the South, and wondered whether I could settle down . . .'

Hughie Gallacher

The two decades which spanned the signing of the Armistice and the start of Hitler's war were a bottle keg of social frivolity, financial depression, widespread unemployment and the menace of impending war against the Nazis. But from a sporting point of view, and particularly from cricket's, it was a golden era, even though the wages of the chieftains were still a joke. In soccer, the Scots proved themselves domestic giants with a shattering 5–1 defeat of England at Wembley in 1928, and it was significant that three of those Wembley Wizards would all be associated with Chelsea.

It was the era of big transfer fees, with the big name clubs buying up players almost hysterically to please their fans – but such plunges into the market did not always prove beneficial, as the Pensioners were to find out. Even with the services of Gallacher, Alec Jackson and Tommy Law, those three Wembley Wizards, in their team in the early 1930s, the Old Unpredictables went on being unpredictable.

With the tansition from silent movies to the talkies, and the advent of glamour movie stars, soccer clamoured for its own star appeal, and Chelsea, as the butt of music hall comedians, looked enviously over to North London where Arsenal, under their legendary manager Herbert Chapman, continued to add to their collection of Cup and League trophies. Finally, when Chelsea went bonkers and tried to buy a Bank of England team at the start of the 1930s, an incensed bishop ranted about the scandal of the 'white slave traffic in footballers'.

In contrast, Chelsea were at their most efficient and consistent in their

The 1920–21 Chelsea team.

The last FA Cup Final to be held at Stamford Bridge before Wembley's take-over – Huddersfield v. Preston North End, 1922.

Above Benjamin Howard Baker, a well-known amateur Corinthian player, was a regular in goal for Chelsea from 1921 to 1926, making 92 League appearances and even credited with scoring a penalty. He was also the England high jump champion, with a record clearance of 6′ 5″.

Alec Jackson, 'the laughing cavalier', endures a skipping session. But his days at Stamford Bridge were not always so high and bouncy.

first full season after the First World War, even though they had been downright lucky to retain a place in the First Division. The club had been relegated in 1915, and a period in the Second Division would have been their lot had not the war suspended football for the duration. And when it was time to start again after all the flag-waving and the return of the lads from the trenches, the First Division was enlarged, and Chelsea and Arsenal were the two clubs to be elected.

Lucky Pensioners – but the honour bestowed on them was to prove in later eras as light as a dinghy's anchor. Unlike Arsenal, who have never allowed themselves to be relegated since, Chelsea bobbed up and down, often narrowly escaping relegation in other years, clinging by their finger-nails. But in 1919–20 they surprised West London by finishing third in the First Division, and going out in the semi-final of the FA Cup against Aston Villa. Had they beaten Villa, they would have appeared on their own ground in the Cup final, one of three to be held at Stamford Bridge between the end of the war and the opening of Wembley Stadium in 1923.

Chelsea's personality player at that time was Jack Cock, another Military Medalist, who came to Stamford Bridge from Huddersfield, and with the reputation for scoring a goal against Ireland – the winner – in the first minute of play. Cock was another great character, not only as a player, but as a music hall singer. The girls at the Granville Theatre, Walham Green used to swoon when Chelsea's groaner warbled love songs up to them from the lights. With his flowing black hair, Cock was the 'dashing' centre-forward of West London, hero of the newspaper cartoonists, idol of Stamford Bridge. Before his transfer to Everton in February 1923, he scored forty-seven goals in ninety-nine League matches, twenty-one of them in that first season 1919–20.

The roaring 1920s were not very happy years for Chelsea, relegated once more to the Second Division in 1924, and unable to win promotion for six years. But while the gay young things in the London West End blew off steam to the Charleston, fun and laughter was not entirely absent from Stamford Bridge either. Another famous character at Chelsea was Benjamin Howard Baker, a world high-jump record-holder, who had taken over from loyal Jim Molyneux 'between the sticks!' Baker had a massive dead-ball kick which would transmit the ball almost into his opponents' penalty-area, and he had a winning way in taking penalty kicks for Chelsea – the only embarrassment being when he missed, and dashed back like a cheetah to man his own goal again.

It may have been a carefree time for the privileged, but for a professional footballer the shackles of the retain and transfer system still prevailed – and wages remained on the breadline level, even for the stars. Andy Wilson, a skilful inside-forward claimed by Chelsea from Middlesbrough in 1923 for £6,500 was not above posing for cigarette advertisements by Stamford Bridge to add a little extra to his eight pounds a week basic wage. Another Chelsea loyalist was Tommy Meehan, a left-half signed from Manchester United. Meehan had to support his wife and four children, as well as his sick father's family – and the strain told. By 1924 Meehan was dead, leaving two impoverished families – but the fans raised fund money to help them.

Chelsea were still in charge of their veteran manager, David Calderhead, who was not to retire until the end of the 1932-33 season. His team, captained by the somewhat tubby Andy Wilson, favoured a popular Scottish style of the time – close passing and clever, clever dribbling. The trouble was that when it came to putting the ball into the net, Chelsea were bluntly useless, mocked by fans and cartoonists alike. The fans, grumbling on that vast slug of terracing, clamoured for goals. But while Dixie Dean, after the change in the off-side law (1925), had beaten the First Division scoring record for Everton in 1928 with sixty goals, the Chelsea players pecked away like starlings on ice. Despite the gifts of Wilson, a long-term Scottish international, promotion was not achieved until 1930.

Then Chelsea went mad. That folklore legend of the north-east, Hughie Gallacher, who scored 132 goals for Newcastle United in 160 matches in five seasons at St James's Park and slotted in some exciting goals for Scotland during the same period, was signed for £10,000; Alec Cheyne, another Scottish international inside-forward, cost £6,000, from Aberdeen; and just to make sure of winning everything, Chelsea paid Huddersfield £8,500 for Alec Jackson, a Scottish idol known as the 'Laughing Cavalier'. Unfortunately, from the point of view of Chelsea spectators, this huge influx of talent proved to be one of the biggest flops of all time. The big, bad South, and notably the night lights of the West End, proved a disastrous diversion. Despite large attendances, Chelsea achieved mediocre results, scoring only ten goals in their first eight games in the 1930-31 season, and by the season's end, the club had to face up to bitchy outside comments – only two other First Division sides had potted fewer goals.

The team looked all right on paper: Sam Millington wasn't a bad goalkeeper, by any means; George Smith lent weight to Tommy Law's dexterity at full-back; Sam Irving, Jack Townrow and Sid Bishop formed a sound half-back line; it was the all-international forward line – Jackson, Wilson, Gallacher, Cheyne and Jackie Crawford – who gave the fans sleepless nights with their unpredictable performances.

What had gone wrong? To begin with, you have to examine the attitude of the men involved at the time and their disturbed morale which led to cases of broken discipline and backroom scenes at Stamford Bridge. Gallacher, the hero of the north-east (like Jackie Milburn, he remains one to this day) was a stocky little athlete, blessed with enough natural gifts and genius to make him the greatest centre-forward of his time. But he also had a quick temper, which could be fanned by a sharp early tackle and could cost a retaliating Gallacher his place on the pitch. Added to such frequent lapses were constant breaches of discipline, absenteeism and spells on the bottle which, after Gallacher's arrival at the Fulham Road club, led to the odd appearance in court for being drunk and disorderly.

Such behaviour showed only too well that Gallacher was suspicious of living in the south, that he found the company he met up with – the hangers-on, the phoneys, two-timing polecats from Stamford Bridge to Piccadilly – too easy to associate with, too hard to shake off. And yet he hadn't even really wanted to leave his beloved club, Newcastle – he was another victim of the system prevalent at the time. This is how he remembered the unhappiness of hearing that Newcastle wanted to transfer the idol of Tyneside:

'A transfer from Newcastle never entered my mind with the close-season holidays (1930) invitingly before me. I had been at home in Scotland only a few hours when there was a knock at the door. Two strangers stood there. They introduced themselves as Mr Claude Kirby, Chelsea chairman, and his chief scout, Jack Fraser. "We've come to take you to Chelsea, Hughie," the chairman said. "That's very nice of you, gentlemen, but I don't particularly want to go, and surely you are overstepping the limit approaching me like this," I replied. Then came the shattering blow. "That's all fixed, Hughie, we've come to terms with United."

'So it had all come out. While I had been playing abroad for my

Hughie Gallacher.

Hughie Gallacher, 'the wee devil', in typically argumentative mood at
Stamford Bridge, as referee Denton rules out his goal against West
Bromwich Albion for off-side. Directly behind him is George Mills, the first
player to score a hundred goals for Chelsea.

This time Gallacher is more successful – side-footing in a goal for Chelsea.
During his Chelsea career he scored 72 goals.

country, the odds had been talked over. I was brought into the deal only at the last moment. You may think I could have refused. I could. But when I felt there was obviously no future for me at Newcastle, there as only one thing I could do.'

Gallacher felt intensely uneasy – as if stabbed in the back by a loyal friend. What would his huge following of Geordies think about it?

'I had a chat with the Chelsea people, but still felt far from easy at the prospect of change. My visitors suggested I accompany them to see the Newcastle representatives. They were waiting at a Glasgow hotel. Now some of my doubts began to clear. "Hughie, me boy, you're in a happy position at Newcastle," I mused. It was obvious that both clubs had set their hearts on the deal, though. Newcastle were keen to release me . . . Chelsea keen to sign me.

'Why Newcastle wanted to let me go I never found out, but with such an attitude, I was bound to leave the club. Better sooner than later. By the time I arrived in Glasgow I knew I was going to move. We started negotiations at eleven o'clock in the morning, and before the day was out I had bounced up half a dozen times, put on my bowler and marched homewards. First, Chelsea officials pulled me back, then it was Newcastle's turn. Everyone had lunch in the same room, the Newcastle folk in one corner, with me seated among Chelsea officials at the nearby table. Afternoon came and went. So did tea-time. Then, at last, the negotiations were settled to everyone's satisfaction. Newcastle were to receive a record £10,000 fee. Chelsea had succeeded in their mission, and I was not displeased. . . .'

So Gallacher joined Chelsea without much financial gain for himself in contrast to lesser, absurdly priced players of today. From Gallacher's point of view, the unease he felt about moving south proved to be justified – the wee man was about to go about his football business in deep, troubled waters.

In their haste to mount a glamour side worthy of the First Division, Chelsea suffered the fate of clubs who over-react to outside pressures. The side which had won promotion that year was a good, steady side – now the arrival of big stars like Gallacher and Jackson led to dressing-room disruptions, petty jealousies, and sheer feebleness when it came to playing football out on the pitch.

As Tommy Law commented in later years: 'I was captain all right, at least until we got on the pitch, then we had eleven captains all telling each other what to do.' Gallacher, of course, did not believe in acting like a reticent mouse, and he didn't like some of Chelsea's training schedules, which involved monotonous jogging round the greyhound track – Hughie liked to get out on the road, where at least there was a change of scenery to relieve the monotony. The trouble was getting Hughie back to Stamford Bridge once he was allowed out. Sometimes he would disappear for days on end, and turn up just in time to catch a train for an important Cup match. David Calderhead's last years as manager could hardly be called an Indian summer, with Gallacher and Jackson around.

Jackson was another enigma, a brilliant, goal-scoring winger who, in the opinion of many who saw him, was a finer performer than Stanley Matthews in his prime. But he also had a university education, and did not suffer fools gladly. He came to London with an enormous reputation, and that he failed to deliver the goods in the penalty box far too often infuriated the fickle Stamford Bridge spectators. Jackson, with his smooth charm and wide smile, was also given special privileges at Chelsea which irritated his team-mates; that he, and not they, could go into the directors' room after a match made them mad. No wonder Chelsea hit rock bottom at times.

Still, Chelsea did manage to reach a Cup semi-final in 1932 – the year Hitler came to power and Harold Larwood invented something called bodyline. By coincidence the opposition was Newcastle United, Gallacher's old club. On his first appearance for Chelsea at St James's Park, in September 1930, Hughie's old fan club had turned up in force and the gates were closed – with 68,000 inside. Half a century on, that remains Newcastle's record attendance, and it will surely do so for ever. Gallacher's new club did not have much luck in the semi-final at Huddersfield. They played neat, attractive football, but the rugged Magpies' defence was too solid for them and finally Newcastle's rapid forwards made sure of a place at Wembley. Newcastle, in fact, won the trophy that year, beating Arsenal 2-1 in the famous 'over the line' final.

All was certainly not well at Chelsea: they only won sixteen out of forty-two games in the 1931–32 season, the rows went on, Tommy Law and Hughie Gallacher refused to re-sign, and Jackson was put on the transfer list with a fee of £4,500 on his head. Jackson eventually moved out of League football after Chelsea refused to reduce his fee – he had played a mere sixty-five games for the Pensioners, some of them sparklers, but somehow Chelsea squandered his wandering talents. Gallacher did

Johnny Jackson.

Andy Wilson.

Sam Weaver.

Eddie Hapgood, illustrious captain of Arsenal and England in the 1930s, hoofs the ball clear at Stamford Bridge as Peter Buchanan of Chelsea flies off his rocking-chair.

rather better, scoring seventy-two goals for Chelsea in 132 League games. Yet things were always on the verge of going wrong at the Bridge when the wee firebrand was around, with or without a hangover.

It was such an atmosphere of turbulence that confronted Leslie Knighton when he took over as manager from David Calderhead, who retired after twenty-five years in 1933. Knighton had been manager at Birmingham – but that had been a smooth ride compared with what he had to tackle at the Bridge. In his memoirs, he summed it up succintly: 'Trouble and then more trouble. That is the football manager's lot, and I had my whack of it at Chelsea – at least in the early days of my work there. When I went to Stamford Bridge, the club were in a very low water financially with a heavy overdraft – I believe it was £12,000. In my six years there the club were enriched by some thirty thousand pounds, besides steadily improving a team of talent. But the work cost me many a weary day and sleepless nights.'

Financial troubles were not Knighton's only problem – Chelsea were up to their usual tricks on the playing fields of England: 'One day they would play like men inspired, and the strongest opposition would go crashing down before them. The next day they would perform like a village side, with missed passes, wild kicks, perhaps scoring through their own goal. They were the most puzzling, yet one of the most attractive clubs that patrons ever had the agony of watching lose a game. In a lifetime of management I had never handled a more intriguing side than Chelsea. I was with them through six sensational years, buying, selling and looking after stars, some of whom, at first, were as temperamental as prima donnas. If my hair is grey, there is a reason for it.'

Knighton failed in trying to get Jackson to patch up his row with Chelsea, but on another front he managed to do what only a young wife called Hannah Gallacher seemed able to do – bring Hughie to heel. 'When I went to Chelsea,' Knighton recorded, 'all sorts of people hurried to warn me that some of the players would take a lot of managing. Among the names particularly mentioned was that of Hughie. I had seen Gallacher's name quoted many times as "football's stormy petrel". Yet I can honestly say that, far from having trouble with him at Chelsea, we became real friends. Gallacher was a perfect little gentleman, always sprucely dressed, always punctilious in looking after himself as a great player should and must.

'The boy who began by kicking a paper ball round a lamp-post in a

Glasgow slum with Alex James was idolized as no other player has ever been. But while playing for Chelsea, Hughie was often badly knocked about, and this affected his temperament. He was a little chap with the heart of a lion, and everyone knew that he was so mad keen on the game that a good hard shove or a charge by a hefty back just after the ball had gone would anger him so much that very probably he would be put right off his game. ...' Despite such rustic attentions, Gallacher controlled his temper – besides putting himself on a milk diet – in helping Chelsea avoid relegation at the end of 1933–34 season.

But the following season, Gallacher was up to his old tricks again, skipping Cup training; Chelsea decided enough was enough, and Hughie was on his way, transferring to Derby, one of six English clubs he played for. 'He scored many picture goals for us before moving along to do the same elsewhere,' Knighton recalled. 'He was one of the great figures of football in my time, and those who saw him play will never forget him.' Nor would Hughie ever forget his turbulent football career, which contained goals, sensations ... money ... or the lack of it. For the eight pounds in winter, six pounds in summer worker: 'If I had my chance again I would not ask for them to be changed – I'd just ask for a little more money.' Gallacher's life came to a premature end after the Second World War, when an eruption of domestic troubles caused him to commit suicide by putting his head under a train.

Apart from Gallacher's rocky run, Knighton had other problems at Chelsea. In the mood of more modern times, Alec Cheyne and Peter O'Dowd suddenly departed to play football in France. Both lived to regret such pioneering decisions, learning that their hosts were wonderfully amicable and hospitable until they started losing – then they blamed the wretched imports. Cheyne and O'Dowd made their own protests against the lamentable state of footballers' wages in England, but in the end they found that the higher cost of living in France, and the poor rate of exchange, hardly left them a working profit. In the end they returned home disillusioned.

Another drama for Knighton was the death of James H. Thorpe, the Sunderland goalkeeper, a few days after a rough-house match against Chelsea at Roker Park on 1 February 1936. Initial Press reports blamed some of the Chelsea players, but they were wrong: Thorpe had been under treatment for diabetes for two years, and it was this which killed him.

Chelsea erected a special platform for the artist Charles Cundall to paint this view of the Chelsea–Arsenal match in October 1935. The gate of 82,905 is still a club record for a home League match.

Vic Woodley, a familiar sight with his flat rustic cap, tipping over a pugnacious shot. He won 19 England caps while at Stamford Bridge in the 1930s.

BIG SIGNINGS – AND MUSIC HALL JOKES – 1919–1939

A Football Association special commission completely cleared the Chelsea players of any blame – but it had been a worrying time for morale. In his six years at Chelsea Knighton produced some talented players, and at one time had two international goalkeepers on his books – Vic Woodley, an eminent performer for England before the Second World War, and John Jackson of Scotland. For a time, the young Woodley kept Jackson in the reserves, but there seems to have been no acrimony or grumbling from Jackson.

But even with so much talent around, Chelsea failed to win anything, and the comics had fun saying so. Knighton might have expected better with, at various times, players like Tom Priestley, a rare wearer of a skull cap; George Mills, the first Chelsea player to score a century of goals; Irish International Joe Bambrick; 'tricky' Dickie Spence, from Barnsley; Jimmy Argue, Sam Weaver, Joe ('Ten Goal') Payne and Billy Mitchell. But honours continued to elude Chelsea, and by now time was running out before the start of Hitler's war.

Knighton said when he left in the summer of 1939, before the first sirens wailed: 'It was the death of three leading directors in three months which helped make the change. I can honestly say I enjoyed my spell at Stamford Bridge immensely, and that I left with the good feeling that I had earned my pay there.' With a new manager in a shrewd Scot, William Birrell, the Chelsea club hoped for a winning season to launch their new beehive-shaped stand, built on stilts at one corner of the ground. But Adolf put a stop to that. Chelsea played their last League game on 2 September 1939.

For the next six years it was khaki, blanco and foot-slogging for the players, and 'guesting' for other clubs. Even so, Chelsea did manage to assemble teams efficient enough to reach the League Cup South finals in 1944 and 1945, losing 3–1 against Charlton in front of General Eisenhower at Wembley in the first, and beating Millwall 2–0 there in front of George VI in the second. In these two matches, the club was captained by a guest player – centre-half Johnny Harris, son of Neil Harris, the old Scottish international, and then with Wolverhampton Wanderers. In post-war years Harris, blessed with a mature football brain, proved himself a real Chelsea man, a loyal servant, a neat, immaculate defender, and won much affection from the fans.

5

High Leaping Tommy

'I felt like a film star at a premiere.'   *Tommy Lawton*

It was during the 1947 chilblain era, that weird, harsh period of post-war austerity when Mr Clem Attlee's Labour government turned everything off and reduced laughter to a squeak, that the feats of one tall, slightly hunched centre-forward warmed the morale of young Chelsea fans, like me, sitting in freezing classrooms. Tommy Lawton was his name, Chelsea's No. 9, England's No. 9, the sharp-shooter with the prodigious leap, the hero with the oval cranium matted overhead with a gauze of black Brylcreemed 'velvet' divided fore to aft at centre with a sheer white parting.

Lawton, scorer of unbelievable goals, champion of speed and finesse; the ace sportsman, holding chin in thumb and forefinger; ambling, hands on hips a moment before a long spring into hostile territory; Lawton, the alarming; Lawton, the flying headsman, master of the sprint, and the clout into the net's far corner; Lawton, England's champion scorer from those lethal Stanley Matthews crosses.

Lawton's achievements at Stamford Bridge revolved around his beautiful goals and glorious headers, and above all that feverish left-foot volley early in 1947 against Arsenal at White Hart Lane in a replayed third round FA Cup tie. The whine of leather off boot was conveyed in a newspaper picture caption: 'A typical left-foot blinder by Lawton from ten yards after shots by Paton and Goulden had been charged down by Arsenal defenders. Note the perfect poise, despite the fierce shot.' Alas, Chelsea were eliminated in the next round in a replay at Derby.

Lawton spent an all too brief two years at Stamford Bridge before his much publicized transfer to the Third Division club, Notts County. But it was goals like the one just described at White Hart Lane which marked him as one of the greatest scoring and heading opportunists of the century. He had signed for Chelsea on 7 November 1945 at a Chester hotel, Everton receiving a cheque for £10,500, which was Chelsea's record transfer fee at the time. Lawton had recently lost his place in the England team after successful years of potting goals in war-time internationals. This, and the fact that his wife was in ill health, had been the decisive factors in Dixie Dean's Everton successor asking for a transfer. Chelsea made the catch, and it was a delighted manager, Billy Birrell, who returned to London in company with the club vice-chairman, Jack Budd.

Lawton could not have signed at a more opportune time for Chelsea – his début in new peace-time football was to be against the famed Moscow Dynamos, who were playing Chelsea in their opening game of what was to be a sensational British tour. After years of bombing and rationing the nation craved new entertainment, and the fact that Lawton was now in the Chelsea team – and, what was more, up against our old Ruskie allies – sent legions of men and women walking down the Fulham Road to the match, that afternoon of 13 November 1945. What happened next was recorded in their memoirs both by Charles Buchan, the former Arsenal and England centre-forward, and later a leading soccer journalist, and by Lawton himself.

The Russians had reacted to the match in fairly typical fashion, the team not turning up for Press interviews at Stamford Bridge, and their newspapers proclaiming that Chelsea had signed Lawton especially to play against the Dynamos. As it was so soon after the War, clubs were still relying heavily on guest players.

Chelsea included in their line-up two Fulham men, defenders Jim Taylor and Joe Bacuzzi, and, like the rest of their Chelsea mates, they were astonished by the crowd scenes confronting them when they marched out of the Stamford Bridge tunnel with the impassive Moscovites. Buchan recalled: 'The gates at Stamford Bridge were shut at least half an hour before the game was timed to start. There were 74,496 officially inside Stamford Bridge, over-flowing the greyhound track, right on to the playing pitch. But with thousands breaking through smashed-down gates, it was reckoned that the actual attendance was around 100,000. The best seats cost ten shillings (50p in today's currency), and the touts were asking, and getting, five pounds for them – which was equivalent to the weekly wage of many a working man at that time.

'When I arrived at the ground there was a milling crowd clustered round the closed gates. Many clambered over at the risk of injury. As the minutes went past I almost gave up hope of getting inside. But somehow I was pushed through a small gate and got to the Press box just in time to see the start. The Russians certainly could play football. They made the ball do the work, moving into positions quickly and serving up a brand that we had not seen in Britain for many years. They drew with Chelsea 3–3. Even though their equalizing goal had a strong suspicion of off-side, they were a grand team, equal to anything we could put against them.'

The Russians, in fact, gave the British football public a foretaste of what the Hungarians would reveal at Wembley a decade later – Chelsea in retrospect did well against the skilful Dynamos. Lawton wrote at the time about what it was like performing in that historic first match of their tour:

'When I arrived at Stamford Bridge it seemed that everybody in London had taken the afternoon off to see the Russians. A huge, surging mob were storming the gates, and mounted police moved slowly among them trying to restore some semblance of order. When eventually the gates were closed, some fifteen thousand would-be spectators were still outside. The inevitable happened. Although the Bridge is a big ground, it wasn't large enough to hold comfortably all who were packed inside. Thousands burst over the barriers and moved across the greyhound track in order to get a closer view of the game when it started.'

Chelsea's new hero, with his heavily Brylcreemed head gleaming, joined his Chelsea colleagues at the entrance of the tunnel: 'When we walked out for the match, a lane had to be made for us through the crowd already lining the pitch. And then came a surprise. When the teams lined up for the National Anthem, we could see that every Russian player carried a posy of flowers. Suddenly, at the word of command from their trainer, they stepped smartly forward and, with a bow but without the flicker of a smile on their faces, they handed each of us a bouquet. I felt like a film star at a premiere. We were glad to hand over our decorations to our luckless trainer, Norman Smith, who went off looking like a harvest festival.

'I had a good look at the Russians as we lined up. They were a young, beautifully built team, rather exotically dressed in Baltic blue shirts, with a large 'D' on the left breast, and darker blue shorts with a white stripe round the bottom, just above the hem. When they stood still it looked for all the world as if they were wearing old-fashioned bathing costumes. But there was nothing old-fashioned about their play. The Dynamos were one of the fastest teams I have ever seen in my life. They went away from the start at a terrific rate, and against our rather disorganized side, with Bacuzzi and Taylor, of Fulham, brought in at the last minute because of injuries to Danny Winter and Dick Foss, showed brilliant teamwork, speed and ball control.

'To be honest,' Lawton recalled somewhat breathlessly, 'the Russians should have been four goals ahead in the first twenty minutes. Only their poor shooting prevented Vic Woodley from doing a bit of back-bending. And then we got started and scored twice in ten minutes.

'In the twenty-fifth minute, Jimmy Bain, our young left-winger, went haring down the line and crossed hard. Tiger Khomich, the Dynamo goalkeeper, and myself went for the ball together, and I managed to force it out of his hands [then allowed in British football] and tap it sideways to Len Goulden [another England international, recently transferred from West Ham]. Len made no mistake. Six minutes later Reg Williams chased a hopeless-looking ball which was in the possession of Stankevich, the Moscow left-back. The defender must have panicked when he saw Williams coming in fast, and, trying to clear, crashed the ball against our player's body, whence it rebounded into the net. That put us two in the lead. Just before half-time, Bobby Russell, our right-half, came out of a sliding tackle with the ball, but was adjudged by the referee to have fouled the Russian centre-forward, and a penalty was awarded. Soloviev, the Russian left-half, and a very good one too, shot about four yards wide – and buried his face in his hands. I should think the crowd surging around and behind the goal had much to do with that miss, if not with the other chances the Russians threw away in that dynamic first half.

'The crowd continued to interfere with the game after the interval and on several occasions had to be pushed back by the police in order that a throw-in or corner could be taken. The Russians "scored" from a rebound from a spectator, but the goal was disallowed. However, with only twenty-two minutes left to play, and Chelsea still leading 2-0, Kartsev, the Dynamo inside-right, scored with a terrific shot from well outside the penalty-area, and four minutes later the Russians were level.

47

Chelsea's wartime success. John Harris receives the 1945 League South Cup
from George VI after the 2–0 win against Millwall at Wembley. Third from
the right is Danny Winter.

A memorable day at the Bridge in November 1945. A packed ground
welcomes the famous Moscow Dynamos.

Among the bashful Chelsea players presented with bouquets by the Russians were captain Johnny Harris (*extreme left*), goalkeeper Vic Woodley (*second from left*) and Tommy Lawton (*third from right*), hair highly Brylcreemed.

The Russians look more stoic. Third from left is Tiger Khomich, a pioneer of aerobatic goalkeeping. The game was a 3–3 draw.

The scorer this time was outside-right Archangelski, and Kartsev's brilliant footwork led up to the goal.

'The Russians played very well together, and it seemed as if they might pull off the game, but Chelsea were still in there fighting, and with only eight minutes left I chased a long, high ball which I managed to head past the advancing Khomich.' A modest description by Lawton – this was one of the maestro's most devastating goals, a typically high leap enabling him to flick the ball past the swarthy Russian goalkeeper from a narrow angle. But, as Lawton remembered, such a moment of personal glory was not enough to give Chelsea an undeserved victory.

'A very bad decision by the referee [Lieutenant-Commander George Clark] made it possible for the Russians to finish all-square. After an attack had been repelled by our captain John Harris, Bobrov, the Dynamo inside-left, was left standing about five yards off-side. Suddenly the ball came whipping back to him, and without any trouble he flashed it past Vic Woodley. The referee gave a goal, which highly tickled the crowd, most of whom had been cheering for the visitors. So the match finished three-all. Although this is the only game I have played against the Russians, [Lawton did in fact play later on the losing side for Arsenal against the Dynamos in the 1950s] I got a fair idea of their play. Make no mistake, they were a very good football team – but not a super side.'

Lawton singled out the Russians' push-and-run team tactics for special praise, but faulted their poor marksmanship. It was the Hungarians who later proved that the Continentals could shoot. But to be fair, four days after playing at Stamford Bridge, the Dynamos did hit ten goals against Cardiff City. Then came a 4–3 win for them against Arsenal on a foggy afternoon at White Hart Lane, and the Russians ended their spectacular tour with a 2–2 draw against Rangers in Glasgow.

Against Chelsea, they had learnt a great deal about English football, and a devastating centre-forward called Lawton. Their captain, Mikhail Semitchastny, made special mention of Chelsea's heading skills: 'The extremely accurate headwork by some players was particularly striking. Take, for instance, Chelsea's centre-forward Lawton, the inside-right Williams, the centre-half and captain, Harris. It is masterly in its precision.' With skills like this, and Lawton leaping like a salmon in the area, Chelsea looked set to make a devastating start to the first post-war season of the recharged Football League in 1946–47.

But though manager Birrell made a sound signing in Tommy Walker,

Lawton demonstrating his heading power against his old club Everton and former colleague Tommy Jones – Stamford Bridge, 1946.

Overleaf: In 1947, when atom bombs were fashionable, the Pensioners greet Liverpool ... and cross swords with the Blades.

THE CHELSEA

F.C. CHRONICLE

Directors: J. H. MEARS (*Chairman*), J. E. C. BUDD,
C. J. PRATT, H. J. M. BOYER, L. J. MEARS

Manager-Secy.: Wm. BIRRELL

Ground: STAMFORD BRIDGE, S.W.6   'Phone: FUL. 3321

Saturday Jan. 4th, 1947	versus LIVERPOOL	PRICE 2d.

WELCOME TO THE FAMOUS **MERSEY "REDS"**
OLD FRIENDS —— OLD RIVALS.

THE RIGHT OF ADMISSION TO GROUNDS RESERVED

THE CHELSEA
F.C. CHRONICLE

Directors: J. H. MEARS (*Chairman*), J. E. C. BUDD,
C. J. PRATT, H. J. M. BOYER, L. J. MEARS
Manager-Secy.: Wm. BIRRELL
Ground: STAMFORD BRIDGE, S.W.6

Saturday May 3rd, 1947	versus SHEFFIELD UNITED	PRICE 2d.

TO LET
VALUABLE ADVERTISING SPACE

Terms from:—The Secretary, Stamford Bridge Grounds, S.W.6.

THE RIGHT OF ADMISSION TO GROUNDS RESERVED

from Hearts, the former Scottish international, a church minister and one of football's gentlemen, Lawton and his colleagues lost too many League games against sides like Manchester United and Wolves, who would soon make their mark. There were too many weaknesses in the Chelsea team, too many veterans, too many novices, but Lawton was capable of making himself a nuisance whenever an opening was handy. He was the supreme artist, the smooth-running opportunist and, for schoolboys outside the gates of Stamford Bridge, a god to look up to and beg for an autograph. By the end of that first full League season (Liverpool claimed the championship), Lawton had broken Chelsea's individual scoring record for the First Division with twenty-six goals in thirty-four games.

On dusty afternoons a group of foxy spivs, star seekers and grubby schoolboys would wait patiently for England's centre-forward to lope through the gates. Lawton often strode in later than the rest. Johnny Harris and the amiable Swiss, Willi Steffen, Tommy Walker, Len Goulden and Dickie Spence were all internationals, but lacked that mystique which separates glamour from the worthy. Lawton would come swinging through the entrance, a towering figure to those of us who had only achieved half our ultimate height. His lighthouse build was enclosed on colder days in a long overcoat, hanging down near his ankles and done up with a loose, flapping belt; the famous greased hair was pasted down over a wide brow, the hero's nose refused to peter out as if fulfilling some sort of navigational function for his subsequent leaps. Beside the former hero of the Folds Road Central School in Bolton, half a dozen hangers-on in slouch hats and untidy pin-stripe suits strained to make their vocal entreaties reach Tom.

Footballers like Lawton were necessary in that barren age; they were monarchs of the bomb-sites, dauphins of conscripts, sporting saints in a nation pastry-eyed from dried milk. 'Tommy, sign my book, please, Tommy – Sign, Mr Lawton – Put your name here, Tom – Score a couple for Uncle Arthur, Tommy.' The hangers-on bustled small intruders aside, as if sensing their own fragile position in the hair-creamed wake of the trudging England centre-forward. This knight in demob armour pushed his way to the dressing-rooms, pausing briefly for a quick chat with Billy Wright or Stanley Matthews waiting to do battle out on the pitch. He could be short with autograph hunters: 'I'm in a hurry, son.' The Lancashire accent was slightly gruff, as if he resented intrusion.

An early League match, in 1946, was against Manchester United –

Chelsea were obliterated by a team recently taken over by a former Scottish international, Matt Busby. Lawton missed a penalty and hardly figured in the match, but later that autumn he showed what separated him from your general, knock 'im in, bash 'em aside centre-forwards. He had something else – an amazing balance, for one thing, and a quickness off the mark which would leave centre-halves trailing behind. Jimmy Greaves gave the same pleasure at Stamford Bridge over a decade later, but it was Lawton who offered it first. But above all there was the headwork from the famous groomed Lawton 'nut', those high bounding leaps a fraction after or before the opposing centre-half, connecting with the ball as the poor rival was going up or already spinning back towards the turf. Billy Wright called Lawton 'the heading maestro – with his eye fixed on the ball, Lawton was always master of it: everyone in England's international team who played with Tommy was impressed with his ability to "place" the ball with his head.'

Lawton's genius, in that first post-war season, was out of context with the general haziness and low standard of the Chelsea side. They were certainly an endearing team, and showed their pre-match enthusiasm by stampeding out on to the pitch with a rush of blue, the big fellow straining to keep up with the wee wingers trying to break Olympic records before the kick-off. Lawton would stand on the edge of the penalty area, rubbing his hands and toeing the ground with an out-stretched boot to test the surface – and surfaces could be pretty awful that season.

He seemed aloof from the others, testing the greasy-capped custodian with wild off-breaks. The players' kit was industrial, to say the least, with heavy bits of everything hanging from neck to ankle, but Lawton always had the appearance of being groomed, as if the gear had been especially ironed to his bones. There was nothing untidy or disorderly about his turn-out as 'star'.

The hated opposition that season were Arsenal, and they figured in an epic, twice-replayed third round cup-tie. Chelsea had improved notably over the Christmas period with the arrival of a Glasgow Press photographer, Johnny Paton, on the left wing. The week before the Arsenal cup-tie Lawton was at his finest against Liverpool, the eventual champions that season. They fielded a strong side, with Sidlow, the Welsh international, in goal, Laurie Hughes at centre-half, Albert Stubbins, that old ginger goal-whacker at centre-forward, and the hero of the Kop,

Harry Medhurst, a much loved Chelsea goalkeeper and later trainer during the FA Cup-winning year of 1970, adopts a snake-charming pose at Highbury in 1947 during a third round replay against Arsenal. Looking on in apprehension: Harris, Ronnie Rooke, Goulden and Macauley.

Tommy Walker.

At the other end Lawton displays his attacking vivacity while evading a chopping tackle by Leslie Compton. Lawton scored Chelsea's goal in a 1–1 draw, but Chelsea won the second replay at White Hart Lane.

Billy Liddell, on the left wing. But it was Chelsea, and Lawton, who astonished and bemused the Merseysiders that damp, misty afternoon, Lawton producing all the skills and centre-forward play which had made him England's regular choice. Memory recalls his first goal, a typical header taken almost at the height of the cross-bar – the downward punch with the famous neck muscles, the ball passing Sidlow by, an elusive blur orbited by some strange, unnatural force. Lawton's second was taken off balance through a crowd of players as he lay back with his head almost touching the turf and his shooting foot thrust forward to connect with the pass. Chelsea won 3–1, and the men of Highbury must have wondered what tragedies lay in wait for them.

In retrospect, Arsenal did very well in the first match at Stamford Bridge. In front of a seventy thousand crowd, Leslie Compton marked Lawton efficiently and Chelsea achieved a draw through a lucky lob from Walker. The two replays were fervent tussles, with Lawton equalizing Ronnie Rooke's goal in the first at Highbury, and winning the second with two devastating goals at White Hart Lane. Tragedy followed in the fourth round: Lawton was in another of his moods when the opposition could be destroyed by his own elusiveness, but luck was not on Chelsea's side. Lawton had one goal ruled out which he said was one of the best he had ever scored. And Raich Carter scored with a ball he undoubtedly handled before shooting. The Stamford Bridge terrace establishment never forgave him for that, and Derby won the replay by the only goal in extra time.

It was during the summer of 1947 that Lawton's rift with Chelsea occurred. Lawton continued to flourish as an international, scoring two goals for the Great Britain side in the 6–0 defeat of the Rest of Europe and four goals for England in the 10–0 rout of Portugal. But his troubles with the club emerged after his reluctance to take part in their tour of Sweden. There had been rumours of dressing-room disorders involving Lawton, but during that long hot summer the rift remained a matter between board and star until the sad news reached the Chelsea fans that the hero had asked for a transfer.

Lawton, of course, was not a handsomely paid star; nobody was in those days. The maximum wage was still twelve pounds a week, but he was able to earn more than the average player through a newspaper column and advertising, and at the time of the transfer request was supposed to be doing quite nicely. The split between the Chelsea board and hero widened. Lawton was determined to go, despite pressure from both club and fan club, but he played in some opening games in the 1947–48 season, and once for the reserves at Highbury in a game which attracted over twenty thousand spectators. And against Derby County, fielding the gifted Billy Steel, he scored a fabulous goal.

Right–half Ken Armstrong, in later weeks to succeed Lawton as a temporary and, for a brief time, a high scoring centre-forward, won the ball and urged it forward to the maestro. The memory projector whirs: Lawton had the ball trapped in an instant, as Leon Leuty lunged ungraciously into the tackle; Lawton sidestepped him and, in one beautiful movement, hit a whizzbang into the top of Townsend's goal. A newspaper caption put the magic in words: ' "That's Torn It!" seems to express Leuty's feelings as he unsuccessfully tries to stop Lawton scoring Chelsea's goal yesterday at Stamford Bridge.'

That goal won the game, and Derby drove away regretting all the misses they had made, while Lawton, who almost scored with an uncanny header in the second half from Walker's lob, disappeared into the dressing-rooms, lost forever to at least one pimply schoolboy praying hourly for a reconciliation.

The row rumbled on into the autumn, when at last Lawton, in face of competition from Stoke City, Blackburn Rovers and Derby County, was transferred to Third Division Notts County for a record twenty thousand pounds. The deed was done – Lawton had got his way. It was a move, he later said, that he lived to regret. Lawton quickly lost his England place, and although he returned to First Division football with Arsenal, via Brentford, the old flair had gone.

6

'Gently Bentley'

After Tommy Lawton's abrupt departure, Chelsea decided they did not possess a first team, and concentrated on boosting their reserve squad, who were doing very well at the top of the Football Combination. It was fun to read in the club programme before first-team matches, which Chelsea lost, about the goal-scoring achievements of the waspish 'Stiffs'. Who, one wondered, was the Chelsea scribe who thought up purple passages like these: 'Westward Ho! to the Drake and Raleigh country, "the glories of Devon" took on a new meaning. Two Devon dumplings for two points were good rations for the day. Although the clouds dropped a deluge, there was nothing of the damp squib about our efforts. Our boys were on top and in no danger throughout.'

And: 'At Swindon the wooden spoonists were all stoked up to lower our flag, and, starting off at top speed, the Railwaymen obviously had no sleepers in their team. Running neck and neck, a timely clearance under pressure found Johnny McKim on the up-line; slipping his guard and veering towards goal, Johnny turned the ball inward for Hughie Billington to shunt the first, close on half-time. On the resumption our boys were forced on the slow line for a period of twenty minutes and our right-of-way was blocked by a checker, but after this breakdown, we got back firmly on the rails again.

'Nationalizing our efforts – a happy band – playing full of confidence – to produce our superior craftmanship, via a defence-splitting through ball from Johnny Galloway, for Hughie to whistle home our second. From a shuttle service of ground level passes, Ken Suttle got up full steam

Billy Hughes, of Chelsea and Wales, depicted on a children's card soccer game in the late 1940s.

Billy Birrell, Chelsea's manager from 1939 to 1952.

Chelsea Pensioners enjoy the pre-match sunshine at Stamford Bridge in the early 1950s.

Roy Bentley, one of Chelsea's more vibrant goal-scorers and prince of heroes between 1948 and 1956. He led the club to their only League Championship victory in 1955.

and, turning past the defences, cracked in a shot with terrific force against their buffers to rebound to Billington to drive home the third and complete his hat-trick for the day.'

Colourful stuff – but it didn't exactly convince the 'vultures' on the Stamford Bridge terraces, taking time off from bread queues on Wednesday afternoons to watch the 'Stiffs'. Galloway ('Go home, *Golloway*') must have been one of the most barracked players ever to appear in a Chelsea shirt, which was odd because he was an elegant footballer.

While the reserves won, and the first team lost, a bright spark thought up the idea of forming a Chelsea supporters' club at the end of the 1940s, because the lads needed an extra cheer or two. But the club refused to recognize the new organization, and it became the Chelsea (Away) Supporters' Club, which meant that, although members wore blue scarves and waved blue-and-white rattles, they were not, in the eyes of their parent club, real supporters at all. They could travel all over the country cheering the Pensioners, but as far as asking favours from the official Chelsea party, like autographs and smiles, they could go packing.

It was a petty time at Stamford Bridge – but matters improved after Chelsea changed their programme and pioneered football's magazine-style programme, edited by that insatiable loyalist, Albert Sewell. The new format was generally adopted by other senior clubs in subsequent years. Manager Billy Birrell, who had found running a flagging club a strain, suddenly discovered that his first team were reviving. Towards the end of 1948, Blackpool, one of the glamour sides of the time, came to Stamford Bridge with the two Stans, Matthews and Mortensen, in the side. A staggering 77,666 fans turned up, and this writer recalls the frightening stampede when he joined three thousand boys taking shelter from terrace pressure on the greyhound track which surrounded the playing pitch. But there were no hooligan distractions as might have occurred today, and the match itself was magic – Chelsea catching up from 3-1 down with seven minutes left to level the scores.

If the match revealed anything, it was that the man Chelsea had signed from Newcastle United as a replacement for Lawton was at least showing a bit of vim, and a taste of his foresight and alacrity in opening up a normally sound defence. Roy Bentley was his name, an almost debonair, shy figure off the pitch – but richly possessed with a football brain, and a flair for sensing openings. It was these gifts that inspired him to knock the breath out of Blackpool in the closing seconds when he sent Johnny

McInnes, a skinny Scot, loping in to beat George Farm for Chelsea's third.

Bentley, a Bristolian, who served with the Royal Navy on dangerous convoy missions to Russia during the war, had joined Newcastle from Bristol City and was a member of the St James's Park club's esteemed forward line including Jackie Milburn and Len Shackleton, which helped them win promotion to the First Division in 1947. At first, Bentley was to experience what other new signings had endured at Stamford Bridge: he couldn't settle down, and the crowd bellowed at him – 'You're no bloody Lawton, Bentley, run off north.' His form suffered through a groin injury, and reserve team football didn't help either: 'I almost felt like packing up,' he was to say later, 'but I knew I had got to fight the odds and justify myself.' And how!

Bentley was to score over a hundred goals for Chelsea, captain the team in their 1955 Championship year, and win a pillowcase full of England caps, including a vital one at Hampden Park in 1950 when he scored England's winning goal against Scotland. Yet all these illustrious moments were well in the future – Bentley still had to prove himself in those years of austerity at the Bridge. But a number of signings, plus the back-up of a promising youth policy pioneered by Billy Birrell, had a heartening effect on results. Suddenly the Pensioners were going places with a side which believed in teamwork and open football, and Birrell had to change his programme notes from the pessimistic to the optimistic – in the 1949–50 season Chelsea had a joyous sleigh-ride to the edge of Wembley Way, only to be knocked into a calamitous icepack by Arsenal.

Chelsea had in the space of a fraction of time produced a team rather than a group of perspiring individualists. It was also a happy team, 'a 100 minute team', as trainer Norman Smith enthused. Harry Medhurst, safe, smallish, but sound in goal; Danny Winter and Billy Hughes, Welsh international full-backs; a strong half-back line in Ken Armstrong, Johnny Harris and Frank Mitchell; and forwards like Billy Gray, Hugh Billington, Jimmy Bowie, Bobby Campbell and Reg Williams and the veteran Len Goulden to compliment Bentley's individual habit of running out on the wings. Bentley's tactics confused static centre-halves of the period, who were drawn out of position to their cost. But if Bentley went 'a-wandering', he could also get back in the goalmouth to make excellent use of his head, which wasn't far behind Lawton's skill in the use of the floated flick. 'Gently Bentley' made goals for Billington and Campbell,

Bentley scoring his most memorable goal for England against Scotland at Hampden Park in 1950. England won through their single goal, and the result was that Scotland did not travel to Brazil for the 1950 World Cup. The goalkeeper is Jimmy Cowan.

Nobody who was there will forget this one – surely one of the most glorious goals ever scored at Stamford Bridge. Roy Bentley (*second from right*) aims a projectile into the roof of Manchester United's net in the FA Cup sixth round in March 1950. *Left to right:* Crompton, behind him Gray who supplied the killing pass, Cockburn, Billington, Carey, Chilton, Aston, Bentley, Warner. Chelsea won a famous victory against the Emperors of the era – 2–0.

One for Chelsea's Chamber of Horrors: after leading 2–0 in their semi-final against Arsenal at White Hart Lane, Chelsea allow the Gunners to force a replay. Here is Leslie Compton (*far right*) heading the second goal from his brother Denis's corner. Chelsea players in the picture (*left to right*): Winter, Medhurst and Harris. Arsenal won the replay 1–0 and went on to win the Cup.

Len Goulden heads a dolly against Manchester City at Stamford Bridge, 1949.

and he scored irresistible ones himself, like his booming angled shot against Matt Busby's Manchester United in the sixth round.

This was one of the most memorable goals in Chelsea's history. With the Pensioners leading 1-0 through a Bobby Campbell goal, and the oppressive talents of United beginning to wear down the Chelsea defence, Billy Gray made a neat back heel out on the edge of the box – and Bentley hit the ball so hard it sizzled past Jack Crompton into the net. This performance was even better than the defeat of Newcastle United in the fourth round, Campbell, that elusive Scot, dashing through the middle from halfway, amazingly keeping his balance on the frozen pitch and beating Fairbrother to make sure of victory.

So Chelsea were in the semi-final against the legions of Highbury – and it was the build-up to this tremendous confrontation at White Hart Lane which prompted a tall, dull-faced man with a narrow jaw to threaten suicide if the Reds beat Chelsea. He was one of thousands queueing up outside Stamford Bridge on a cold, spring morning in March 1950. 'If Chelsea lose next week, I'll put my head in a gas oven, honest,' he said. 'Chelsea can't lose. Look at what they did to Manchester United. They'll slaughter them,' a sallow youth replied in the milky dawn.

'They'll win all right,' said the gas man. 'I've been watching them since 1920 and this is their best yet. Gallacher, Wilson, Mills – you can 'ave 'em. Bentley's the bloke. Now look at it this way, his speed and shot, he's got it. Leslie Compton won't see him. But I'm still telling you that if Chelsea lose I'll put my head in a gas oven.' It brought a laugh from the massed queue. They had waited hours to buy tickets, spreading back towards Walham Green tube station, faces chilled by the cold. 'What d'you think the score will be, then?', another weasel-faced youth asked. 'Chelsea 3, Arsenal 0.' The gas man hung the 0 in the morning air, savouring its round loop. 'Roy'll put two in the net before Joe Mercer's got his tits warm. George Swindin will be lying there as if he's kicked the bucket with the ball in the net.' 'What will you do if we lose, then?' 'I'll put my head in a gas oven.' The gas man got a pair of tickets but what happened after the calamities to come will never be known. But in the meantime he and his friend made their way on a sunny Saturday to watch the two London stags lock their horns.

Outside windy White Hart Lane, an accordionist played *Music, Music, Music* (the hit tune of the time) and thousands wearing blue-and-white scarves waited for the gates to open. The White Hart Lane pitch looked like a sanded estuary, the band thumped out *Colonel Bogey*, and these were the teams:

Arsenal: Swindin; Scott, Barnes; Forbes, L. Compton, Mercer; Cox, Logie, Goring, Lewis, D. Compton.

Chelsea: Medhurst; Winter, Hughes; Armstrong, Harris, Mitchell; Gray, Goulden, Bentley, Billington, Williams.

With Bowie and Campbell injured, Chelsea brought Reg Williams and, surprisingly, the veteran Goulden into the side – decisions which were to have mixed blessings. A peep from referee, Reg Leafe, and one of the most amazing of games in the history of Chelsea Football Club commenced, with more than seventy thousand roaring on their beloved teams.

Subsequent events were pure *Boy's Own Paper* stuff. With Chelsea playing fluent, unhurried football, and Goulden, the old fox, playing a leading part, the redoubtable Arsenal defence began to quiver.

In the twentieth and twenty-fifth minutes, Bentley duly found them out with two lethal goals: the first a beautiful lob over Swindin's head, the second a glided header inside the near post. Chelsea were at Wembley, surely – nothing could stop them playing the first real Wembley final in their history. But now Pandora emerged on the scene with her famous box, and what happened on the brink of half-time changed the course of the game – and the appetites of Chelsea supporters for months to come. Alan Hoby, a Chelsea citizen and supporter described the scene in the *Sunday Express* next morning: 'A goal so freakish that it should be permanently installed in the Chelsea Chamber of Horrors smashed the Pensioners' dream of marching straight through to Wembley. Thirty seconds before half-time Arsenal, two goals down and with defeat sneering them in the face, forced a corner. Then the North London "miracle" happened. Without apparently a pinhead hope, right-winger Freddie Cox, taking the kick with the inside of his right foot, sliced over a ball which literally screamed towards goal. Even then it did not seem possible for Arsenal to score. But at the last split second the ball curved in and rocketed into the net. The wind helped it in. Afterwards Medhurst, the Chelsea goalkeeper, said: "The ball was in the net before I touched it." I give this goal in such detail because in my view it was the turning-point of this highly dramatic semi-final.'

Hoby was correct – Chelsea fell back on the defensive in the second

CHELSEA
FOOTBALL CLUB

F.A. CUP—SIXTH ROUND
CHELSEA v MANCHESTER U

Saturday, 4th MARCH, 1950

KICK-OFF 3-0 p.m.

Official Programme 6d

STAMFORD BRIDGE GROUNDS LONDON S.W.6

THE RIGHT OF ADMISSION TO GROUNDS IS RESERVED

Chelsea, with editor Albert Sewell, were the first to pioneer a new-style programme in the late 1940s. In this edition a rising young actor, Richard Attenborough, later to become a club director, congratulates Johnny Harris during Chelsea's 1950 Cup run which took them to the semi-finals. Billy Hughes grins in the background.

In the spring of 1951 Chelsea amazingly escaped relegation by ·044 of a goal. In one of their crucial last matches Bert Williams, the Wolves and England goalkeeper, was beaten by a disputed goal by Ken Armstrong (*above*), and by this explosive penalty from Roy Bentley (*below*).

half, Williams missed an open goal for them, and Arsenal fought back with courage and tenacity. Although ordered not to go up by his captain, Mercer, Leslie Compton disobeyed, and headed a stunning goal from his brother Denis's corner kick. And near time, Denis almost scored the winning goal with a header which clipped the bar: 'That was an amazing one,' Denis mused in retirement years over a glass of hock. 'I actually dived and caught the ball perfectly – a novel act for me . . . It would have been a wonderful winner.' And so the gas man mourned, and it was a saddened Bentley and Chelsea who regrouped at Tottenham for the Wednesday replay. This time it was Cox again, in injury time, who put a thorn in Chelsea's throbbing side with a left-foot swinger. 'I moved along the Chelsea line and couldn't help thinking it was like an officer inspecting a parade,' he told Desmond Hackett afterwards. 'No one moved. Then I saw the goal. . . .'

Cox's goal, which took Arsenal to Wembley and victory over Liverpool, was a belt in the face for Chelsea. With a Cup final place literally there for the taking, two acts of sheer larceny by Arsenal sent morale plummeting at Stamford Bridge. Chelsea started losing again. The situation was so bad that towards the end of the following season the club were in danger of being relegated. With four games to go, Chelsea were four points behind Sheffield Wednesday, and six behind Everton. With Chelsea in such dismal form the task looked helpless, even to their most fervent supporters. After twenty years Chelsea were on their way out of the First Division.

And yet, who in their right mind has ever safely made an accurate forecast about Chelsea? In the first of the four matches, against Liverpool, Chelsea brought a burly young Scot, Bill Robertson, into goal for his first senior match. Robertson was such a bundle of pre-match nerves that trainer Norman Smith had to dose him with brandy, but once on the field, 'Big Bill' did well, and Bobby Smith, a bluff, square-shouldered product from the Chelsea youth scheme, knocked in the winning goal. In the next match Chelsea beat Wolves at Stamford Bridge with a disputed Bentley penalty and a goal by Armstrong after he clearly handled the ball. Luck was running Chelsea's way – now they had a chance to stay up – and on the following Saturday Fulham were beaten 2–1 at Craven Cottage, the home crowd singing *Dear Old Pals* as Fulham missed one open goal after another.

So, for the final game at Stamford Bridge against Bolton, Chelsea

Bobby Campbell pressurizes Lloyd of Tranmere in the FA Cup fourth round at Stamford Bridge, February 1952.

Bobby Smith scores one of the goals in his memorable hat-trick against Leeds in the FA Cup sixth round replay at Villa Park in 1952. Second from right, somewhat forlorn, is the great John Charles. Chelsea went out in the semi-final, again after a replay against Arsenal.

PERSONALITY PROFILE—No. 14

Norman Smith, in post-war years ever loyal with the sponge, caricatured in a 1951 Chelsea programme.

were given a reasonable chance of staying up. Forty thousand marched along the Fulham Road to cheer the Blues on – and in the end Chelsea were granted the narrowest of reprieves. Two headers by Bentley, and another two goals by Bobby Smith, got Chelsea a 4–0 lead, and nails were busily chewed before the result of the Sheffield Wednesday match came through. It eventually did – 6–0 to Wednesday, but that half-dozen was not enough to stop Chelsea escaping relegation by an incredible ·044 of a goal. In fact, the last three clubs finished with thirty-two points each, but Chelsea's superior goal average kept them breathing – sheer Houdini stuff.

Another undistinguished League season in 1951–52 was nearly compensated for by an elusive appearance in the Cup Final, but, ironically, it was Arsenal again who put paid to that dream with another semi-final replay win at White Hart Lane, Cox again making his damaging point. But this Chelsea, in retrospect, were nowhere near as good as the 1950 side. At the end of that season, Billy Birrell decided to call it a day – not the most inspiring of managers, but a kindly man, conscious of the problems that can afflict footballers. His successor was the Southampton-born Ted Drake, in his playing hey-day a net-bursting centre-forward for Arsenal and England, and recently manager of Reading. He came to Stamford Bridge asking the Chelsea fans to be 'kind' to their team. He promised rebuilding – and the making of a winning team. Many managers have said that, but in Drake's case the pot of gold was nearer being found than even he can have dared to hope.

7

The Golden Jubilee Championship

Ted Drake inherited a staff of more than fifty professionals when he took over Chelsea in 1952 – but he promptly dismissed the club's oldest servant, the famous Pensioner mascot. 'He has done great service to Chelsea, but I do feel we need a modern image' was the gist of Drake's reply to the hundreds of protesting letters.

The first team still had Roy Bentley, but men in surrounding positions were plainly suffering from a lack of confidence. In Chelsea's first League match under Drake at Stamford Bridge, the crowd booed unmercifully a well-meaning but over-strung Irish forward, Jimmy D'Arcy, because of his inability to find the Derby net. 'The torment of D'Arcy began in eighteen minutes when his header, so thoroughly deserving to be a goal, hit a post,' Desmond Hackett wrote in the *Daily Express*. The fans wanted a new winning deal straight away, not realizing that the kindly Drake, a Hampshire man with a heavy burr, had to assemble a team around Bentley first. But the crowd grumbled away, and kept grumbling even though they could not always see what was going on. It was an era of winter smog – the thick, oily kind that enveloped the Fulham Road and restricted visibility to a few yards. Alan Ross, the poet, and *Observer* football correspondent at the time, came along to analyse Drake's new team – but found all he could see was the odd smudge of blue. Yet he still had room to do a thorough knocking job:

'Chelsea and Stoke City, once again clutched in an octopus-like struggle in the murky depths of the First Division, played a goal-less draw at Stamford Bridge yesterday. Chelsea had picked up their first point since 25 October in a drawn game at Stoke on Boxing Day, so they had no reason to be discontented over their holiday haul. At the present rate, however, one, if not both, of these teams will go down to the Second Division next season, and neither, it must be admitted, look at the moment good enough to remain where they are.

'If the quality of play at Stamford Bridge was negligible, this match was nevertheless a memorable visual experience. It began in a light veering fog, which laid a transparent silky screen across the ground. Although the players remained coated with a curious clinging dew, most of the play was clearly visible throughout the first half. Sometimes a thick wave of fog made the stadium seem like a film construction of a gas attack for a World War I epic; then, in a clearer spell, the teams moved in a kind of ballet among the clouds, the ball often lost from sight but whole sequences of intricate passing preserved from the fog and given a special beauty.'

Ross was not the only writer enraptured by the Stamford Bridge setting, if not the team. David Sylvester, the art critic, wrote a piece on Chelsea, 'the romantics', and Arsenal, 'the realists'. Johnny Minton, the painter, and Laurie Lee, the poet, joined friends on Saturdays at the Bridge, where laughs were paramount, quality frail. Chelsea were a music hall joke again.

At the end of the 1953 season, the club barely escaped relegation – and the future looked ominous. Until, that is, the moment came when Chelsea forgot to lose, and went on winning. Drake had made some sound signings since his arrival, and none better than Johnny McNichol from Brighton and Hove Albion. McNichol, an elusive Scot, with much of Charlie Cooke's flair in later years for spying an opening in a premature split second, began to experience more and more occasions when his understanding with Bentley intrinsically bullseyed. They were the perfect foil to each other's varying styles: Bentley, the ubiquitous wanderer and champion goal-scorer; McNichol, the mole behind him, working destructively at opposing nerve centres.

The form of Eric Parsons was also a revelation. He had been transferred to Chelsea in November 1950 from West Ham, but that lack of confidence which afflicted many of the club players at the time restricted his power play on the right wing, and kept him in reserve team football – which his talents did not deserve. It was not until the 1953–54 season, when a long spell without defeat took Chelsea up the table to a respectable final eighth place, that Parsons, or 'The Rabbit' as he was known

Two contemporary managers in confrontation at the Bridge – 1952. Ronnie Allen (*second from left*), turns for a handshake from WBA's Johnny Nicholl after putting the ball past Chelsea's goalkeeper Bill Robertson from close range. Displaying his grief (*second from right*) is Ron Greenwood. Allen returned to manage Albion in 1981. Chelsea's Number 3 is Syd Tickridge.

Bill Robertson manages to deflect a Wolves whizz-bang at Molyneux in 1953, but he cannot prevent Wolves scoring eight goals – still the record League defeat for Chelsea.

Ted Drake.

affectionately by the Stamford Bridge fans, blossomed into a threatening, up the wing and at them runner. There are countless snaps in the memory of Eric zipping up the wing, and Bentley billowing the net from another accurate low centre from 'The Rabbit'.

At this time, Drake was making subtle changes in the side, and by the start of the 1954-55 season (Chelsea's half-centenary year) it seemed the club, a talented, if not great side, were ready to win something. But with teams like Manchester United and Wolves around, it was a bold punter who backed them to win their first League championship. That it finally happened in most magical style on a spring afternoon at Stamford Bridge was the result of hard teamwork and fitness by Drake's squad. Most of them had either served in the war, or were currently still doing National Service, like left-winger Pte Frank Blunstone RAMC, a close-cropped young import from Crewe Alexandra. There was something almost military about the Chelsea team, boots highly polished, hair well combed, shoulders back, chests out – the boys got down to work with a zest.

In goal for the first half of the season was the faithful, square-jowled Bill Robertson; there was no reason to suppose he would be shifted until an ankle injury in training made him miss a match – but Charlie (Chick) Thomson was such a bold deputy that he kept his place for the rest of the season. The full-backs, Stan Willemse and Peter Sillett, if sometimes caught square by players with the ability to run like Johnny Berry of Manchester United, were nevertheless reliable and hard-kicking centurions. They had formed a steady partnership by the time the season reached its critical stage, and an able twelfth man and full-back was none other than Johnny Harris, who played enough matches to qualify for a championship medal.

The half-back line proved a winning factor – Ken Armstrong performing so positively that he would gain an England cap against Scotland at Wembley, Ron Greenwood, a future West Ham and England manager, playing steadily at centre-half until replaced by the colossal Stan Wicks from Reading, an underrated player, whose form, until his premature and stifling injury, grew progressively more advanced and less pleasant for rival centre-forwards. At left-half emerged the red-haired amateur from Walthamstow Avenue, Derek Saunders, a tough tackler and keen distributor of the ball, who replaced a fine club man, Bill Dickson.

The forward line based itself on smothering attacks built along the wings, with Bentley ready to use his head to nod in a rain of centres from

Snow at Stamford Bridge. Lithograph by Alistair Grant.

Roy Bentley's 100th First Division goal for Chelsea in October 1954 against WBA was one of many personal highlights leading up to the League Championship.

Parsons and Blunstone. McNichol worked the engine-room at inside-right, and Les Stubbs, at inside-left, had a shot like a mule's kick. There were more than useful substitutes for the forward positions – Jim Lewis, another amateur from Walthamstow Avenue, was available to fill in when Blunstone was injured, and Seamus O'Connell, yet another amateur, came down from Bishop Auckland.

O'Connell's debut for Chelsea in the autumn had an element of the fairy story about it – but first to Chelsea's assault on the League championship, which in October, at least, seemed a negligible one. The club had got off well enough with Bentley sniffing for the first of the twenty-one goals he would score that season. But by October, they were falling down the table, and then one point from five matches levered them down to twelfth place. O'Connell's debut was on 16 October, Manchester United coming to town with a sprinkling of the future Busby Babes. O'Connell arrived for the occasion with his boots wrapped up in a brown paper parcel – he could scarcely have imagined what lay in store for him, or the feverish 56,000 crowd.

Most of those who have followed Chelsea before and since the war would not disagree about this game being the most exciting ever played at Stamford Bridge – to say it had everything is borne out by the scoreline, which beat a tattoo after United took the lead. When Chelsea equalized, goals came with ping-pong rapidity – now Chelsea took the lead, then it went 2-2, 2-3, 2-4, 2-5 (United thoroughly in control by now), 3-5, 3-6, 4-6, 5-6. O'Connell had the misfortune to score a hat-trick on that golden afternoon and still finish a loser, but there was pride in every player at the end, and handshakes all round. Thirty-two minutes of this electric game contained eight goals – 'Wow,' a watching American said on the terraces. 'Some ball game!'

Despite the disappointment of that desperately 'close run thing' in favour of United, Chelsea derived heart from their come-back against a highly accomplished side. With English football all agog about Hungarian tactics after the two thrashings handed out by the national side against England, a full house at Stamford Bridge licked their lips in anticipation of a classic from Chelsea's friendly against Red Banner. But a drawn game fell below expectations – the Hungarians in this match showing they could make mistakes like anyone else. Two penalties were conceded in Chelsea's favour, John Harris missing both, and to add to this indignity, he gave one away as well – but the Hungarians fluffed that one, too.

Things picked up for Chelsea in the League and by the New Year they were lying handily in fifth position, Peter Sillett showing, after previous failures in other matches by Harris and Bentley from the spot, that he was ready to assume the penalty-taking responsibility with a whizzbang into Bolton's net. By the spring, Chelsea had reached a position where the taking of the League championship had become rather more accessible than the faraway mountain shrouded in mist it had been before. It was possible, indeed it was; Ted Drake's class showed over the last thirteen matches that they were capable of sustaining their consistency, losing only two of these games – one against Aston Villa, and the other against Manchester United when the title was already won.

Older Chelsea supporters will remember the thrill of those last games, with victories over Charlton, Sunderland – when Drake tried out a future England forward, Peter Brabrook, with positive results – and over Tottenham at White Hart Lane. Chelsea were by now four points clear of Wolves at the top of the table, and going for the finish. The trouble was that the fans were unable to read about their team's successes in the newspapers – there was a Fleet Street strike on at the time, which even blanked out the resignation of Sir Winston Churchill as Prime Minister.

Even so, Chelsea went eagerly about their business, and by the time the papers appeared again, they were almost crowned kings of the First Division. The really important match Chelsea had to win was against title rivals Wolves at Stamford Bridge on a sunny afternoon in April. It was Easter Saturday, and Stamford Bridge was stretched at the seams with seventy-five thousand inside. Wolves paraded their famous stars in force: Billy Wright, Bert Williams, Johnny Hancocks, Roy Swimbourne and Ron Flowers included. They were a great side, a winning side, having recently beaten Spartak (Russia) and Honved (Hungary) in friendly matches. A win by Wolves that afternoon would have cut Chelsea's lead at the top of the table to one point – and put them in a good position conclusively to overtake the West Londoners. Wolves knew all about Chelsea – less than two years before they had crushed them 8–1.

There was an unforgettable roar as Chelsea took the field, blue balloons soared in the air, and grown men quivered with expectancy. Could Chelsea really do it? The side had been out of form the previous day in a drawn match against Sheffield United, but on this occasion, raising their game against the men in old gold, they produced dollops of the fast, adventurous football which had already taken them so high in the League. Bert Williams leapt and twisted to keep out ferocious shots by Parsons, Bentley and Sillett before half-time, but he should have been beaten with far easier chances by Bentley and O'Connell. The minutes ticked by, with Swimbourne limping from an early injury. Wolves held on – a point would be more than useful to their championship aspirations. Then Chelsea at last got the break their attacking football had deserved. With fifteen minutes left, O'Connell unleashed a stinging drive towards the top corner, and Williams, beaten totally, watched his captain, Wright, punch the ball behind. At first, the referee gave a corner. The Chelsea players raved, the crowd raved, the stadium frothed and heaved; it took some time before Mr J. W. Malcolm deemed a word with a linesman was necessary, but at last he trudged over to the touchline.

Back came Mr Malcolm, possibly enjoying the drama he had caused – then out came a long, rigid finger pointing at the Wolves spot. Now in a deadly hush, it was time for the burly Peter Sillett to do his duty. Years later, his brother John, who was also on Chelsea's books, recalled what Peter had said about that moment of screeching responsibility: 'Peter said it was the most terrifying moment of his playing career – he had to make the long walk up the pitch and put the ball on the spot. Some of the Chelsea players couldn't face the spectacle, and turned away. Peter saw Bert Williams standing in goal as big as a ruddy elephant, he stepped back, moved forward three paces and gave the ball everything he had. Williams dived – but the ball hit the net like a steam-engine out of control.'

It was the killing match-winner, although Chelsea had some luck late in the game when a shot by little winger Hancocks, who had moved to centre-forward, beat Thomson but hit a post. Mr Malcolm blew his whistle, the Chelsea crowd rejoiced. Now for the title!

Two more games remained, against Portsmouth at Fratton Park, a drawn affair, in which Les Stubbs was unlucky to have a ferocious, close-range goal ruled out, and the grand finale against Sheffield Wednesday at Stamford Bridge. By now the Fleet Street presses were rolling again and eager to tell the story of Chelsea's first championship. Sheffield Wednesday were beaten 3–0, but the home crowd had to wait fifteen minutes for the Cardiff–Portsmouth result to come through. At last it did, a 1–1 draw, confirming Chelsea were champions in their Golden Jubilee Year. The crowds massed in front of the directors' box; somebody

Teamwork by Chelsea's League Championship-winning half-back line –
Saunders (6); Armstrong (4); Wicks (5).

Chelsea's captain Roy Bentley applauds with his team-mates as the manager Ted Drake makes a kind reference to the overall contribution of Eric 'The Rabbit' Parsons (*second from left*) as the club celebrates victory in the 1955 League Championship.

The champions pictured at Old Trafford the week after clinching the title.
Standing (*left to right*): J. Oxberry (Trainer), S. Willemse, K. Armstrong,
P. Sillett, S. Wicks, C. Thompson, D. Saunders, J. Harris; seated: E. Parsons,
J. McNichol, R. Bentley (Captain), E. Drake (Manager), S. O'Connell,
F. Blunstone.

with a blue-and-white scarf warbled 'Only the Blues, to carry me by ...'; the players came out in tracksuits, towels wrapped round their necks. It was a quiet, almost dignified occasion ... Joe Mears, the owlish chairman, came to the microphone and spoke up for everyone: 'I would like to thank everybody for the wonderful ovation you have given us today and for your support all through the season. It is not for me to say more than a few words. You want to hear from Roy and the boys, and from the one and only Ted.'

Then up stood Ted Drake, and gave the happy crowd a broad Hampshire smile: 'At the start of the season I was asked if we would win the Cup. I thought we might, but I thought we had a greater chance of winning the Championship. I congratulate all the boys and every one of my staff, office, training and playing. Right throughout they are one and all CHELSEA.' Then shy, unassuming Roy Bentley came forward, the captain and architect of victory: 'On behalf of the boys, thank you all. There is no need for me to say how pleased we are to win the Championship, but we are pleased, too, for your sakes, because you have been behind us in other years when we needed your support. From the bottom of our hearts thank you very much. ...' Cheers all round.

Now came the champagne, the backslapping and optimism for the future. As on so many other occasions in Chelsea's history, however, Pandora's box was due for another opening. But nothing should be taken away from that most glorious season in Chelsea's history, a season in which all four of their teams captured top prizes. The magic one, the First Division championship, was won with fifty-two points – a lowish figure – with Wolves runners-up with forty-eight, ahead of Portsmouth on goal average. Chelsea teams also won the Football Combination – Division 1, the Metropolitan League, and the South East Counties League (Juniors).

Chelsea paraded the Championship trophy in front of their fans at the start of the new season – then slipped into hibernation for the rest of the decade. As far as football was concerned Chelsea remained detached from the honours game, meekly declining the chance of competing with Real Madrid, Reims and other great teams of the period in the first European Cup competition in 1955–56, after the Football League made a pompous fuss about possible fixture congestion. It was the Busby 'Babes' of Manchester United who became pioneers for England in this competition a season later. Alas, it was to be a short expedition, because the Munich air crash all but destroyed Matt Busby's team a year later.

The cartoonist Tom Webster records Chelsea's long-awaited moment of glory.

CHELSEA, by winning the League Championship on Saturday, put all the funny men out of business.

LABOUR EXCHANGE

GONE! are those glorious days when, if Chelsea scored, excursions were run from all parts of Gt Britain to enable people to gaze at the ball in the net.

GONE! are those festive times when a Chelsea Director had to look the other way for 90 minutes.

STILLED for ever are those throbbing throats exhorting CHELSEA to "WAKE UP!"

In the air once more is the pigeon which —

— at one time suffered from foot-rot through not being released with glad tidings.

At 4·45 p.m. the football which got CHELSEA "home" on Saturday rolled pleasantly on the pitch. We understand that it is being given to the nation, provided —

— it doesn't burst with pride.

Tom Webster

Now CHARLES BUCHAN takes up the story—
GAME CHELSEA WIN RECORD FOR DRAKE

Chelsea .... 3 Sheffield Wednesday 0

CHELSEA not only created a record for the club by winning their first major League honour in their Jubilee Year but also set up a record for manager Ted Drake.

The former Arsenal and England centre-forward is the first man ever to play in a First Division championship side and later manage a team that carried off the title.

After Chelsea had beaten Sheffield Wednesday 3—0 at Stamford Bridge, Mr. Drake said : "Of course, I am tremendously pleased But I am happier for the sakes of players like Ken Armstrong and Johnny Harris who have given long and splendid service."

I think Tommy Law, Scottish international and former Chelsea left-

ALL YOUR RACING IS ON PAGE 11

international So we may nave the League champions and runners-up holidaying in Paris together in three weeks' time.

THE GOLDEN JUBILEE CHAMPIONSHIP

About the time of Prime Minister Anthony Eden's ill-fated Suez expedition, and the launching of Rock 'n Roll by the Chelsea Set along the Kings Road, Ted Drake decided he was going to raise a kindergarten and build a new team. The old hands moved on, including loyal Ken Armstrong to New Zealand, and loyal Roy Bentley, prematurely – and shabbily, many Chelsea fans felt at the time – to Fulham. Drake, with an eye cocked towards Old Trafford, plumped for youth from the lower echelons of the club – with one major addition, Reg Matthews, a nervous, chain-smoking goalkeeper transferred from Coventry for a new record fee for a netminder.

Matthews came to the Bridge with a healthy reputation for keeping the ball out of the net, and England caps to show for it. But his inconsistency during 135 appearances hardly helped the youngsters in front of him. One week he would be the best goalkeeper in the country; the next, the worst. But that was Chelsea all through at the time. New faces, new fluffy chins: Peter Brabrook, David Cliss, Mel Scott, Tony Nicholas, Ron Tindall, were given regular places. And last, but not least, the greatest English goal-scoring machine of all time – one James (Jimmy) Greaves.

Greaves was discovered in 1954 by chief Chelsea scout Jimmy Thompson, playing schoolboy football in East London. Thompson rang up Drake after the 6–5 epic against Manchester United to find the Chelsea manager in a state of near collapse after the ding-dong. 'I've just seen the most exciting game of my life,' Drake said breathlessly. 'And I've seen the player of a lifetime,' replied Thompson, who brought the stripling along to Stamford Bridge and introduced him to Drake with the words, 'Meet the Champ!'

With his long, Alex James shorts, cropped hair, firm but slim jaw-line and totally boyish physique, Greaves could hardly have struck terror through the minds of large Tottenham defenders when he made his début for Chelsea at White Hart Lane on the first day of the 1957–58 season. Until the former apprentice put foot to the ball, and then the picture changed – a genius was in song. Danny Blanchflower quickly joined an appreciative chorus of approval afterwards for the seventeen-year-old wizard, who scored a late equalizer for Chelsea: 'Jimmy Greaves gave the greatest show I have ever seen from a young player on his League début, and I have seen the juvenile performances of soccer starlets Johnny Haynes and Duncan Edwards. The boy is a natural. He is the greatest youngster I have ever played against.'

A genius, indeed, and worthy of praise from a talented Irishman he would team up with for several years to such effect at Tottenham. Meanwhile, in those hurly-burly days, Greaves went about scoring goals with a vengeance; superb goals, rampant goals, goals a-plenty, including five at Preston, five at home to West Bromwich and another five against Wolves, which virtually put an end to Billy Wright's long career.

Greaves had the gift, the deadly gift, for finding unseen space, and making it pay; his darting bursts and solo runs earned him 124 goals in 157 League appearances for Chelsea between 1957 and 1961. He was the hero of Stamford Bridge, and yet the club, as in the days of Lawton, did not quite know what to make of it all. They had in their midst a scoring genius, a player Tony Pawson described as 'simply unique as a goal-scorer', but around him, the texture was frayed. Thus Greaves, with his superb balance, banged in the goals, and Chelsea duly let in goals at the other end.

Greaves recalled those funny, sometimes futile days at Stamford Bridge in his own memoirs. Discipline was lax, laughs many, results fickle.... 'We were labelled "Drake's Ducklings" and had more potential than any other team I have ever played for. But you need experienced players to help draw out the potential, and we were just a bunch of kids playing it off the cuff and often coming off second best. It was like being at Butlin's, a real holiday camp atmosphere. Our lack of success did nothing to harm the dressing-room spirit and even in defeat you would find us falling about laughing at things that went on at the club. We were still kids waiting to grow up....'

Some of the matches were a comedy of errors, and Greaves looked back on them with a chuckle: 'One of the best laughs at Chelsea was during a League match with Everton after they had scored against us. Actually we scored it for them and I still rate it one of the all-time unforgettable goals. If there had been action replay machines around in those days I am sure they would still be showing it as a comic classic. A long shot from an Everton player slipped under the body of Reg Matthews. Reg scrambled up and chased the ball, hotly pursued by Peter Sillett, who thought he had a better chance of clearing it. They pounded neck and neck towards our goal. Reg won the race and then, instead of diving on the ball, elected to kick it away. He pivoted beautifully and cracked the ball dead centre – straight into the pit of Peter Sillett's stomach. The ball rebounded into the back of the net and Peter collapsed

Jimmy Greaves, scorer supremo, shooting at goal against Spurs at Stamford Bridge.
Greaves in tackling confrontation with his renowned England partner Johnny Haynes at Craven Cottage. Haynes's Fulham colleague on the left is Jimmy Langley.

holding his stomach. The rest of us collapsed in laughter.' Somehow, the show went on without Chelsea being relegated.

In retrospect, what a pity Greaves never linked up with Bobby Smith at Chelsea – but Smith had long gone to Spurs, and the pair would not get together until a few years later, when they played so effectively with each other for England, and, of course, Spurs. Greaves regarded Smith 'as the perfect foil for me ... he had the strength and tenacity of two men, could win the ball on the ground or in the air and was a master at laying the ball off to team-mates either side of him.' Not that Greaves's goal-scoring suffered at Chelsea, but an older head like Smith's might have helped in a novice side.

Greaves's stay at Stamford Bridge ended with that ill-fated £80,000 transfer to AC Milan, done he admits for 'mercenary reasons'. As he was a £20-a-week footballer at the time, you could not exactly blame him for making the decision. At first he tried to 'wriggle out of the deal', especially when Chelsea's chairman, Joe Mears, said the club would be prepared to pay him £100 a week. But AC Milan offered Greaves a new bait – a fifteen thousand pounds signing-on fee. It was too much to resist, Greaves signed.

The fans carried their hero off the pitch at Stamford Bridge 'as if I were the FA Cup' after his last match, in which he scored all Chelsea's goals in a 4–3 win against Nottingham Forest. His club had made a profit of £79,990 from the transfer of their former apprentice, originally paid just over four pounds a week. It was a sad ending, with Greaves suspended by the club and missing an England cap because he refused to go on a tour to Israel.

Greaves was now facing, in his own words, 'days of wine and woes', but that is another story. It is best to remember here his joyous exhibitions in the blue shirt, and goals like the one against Birmingham when he beat everybody down the middle, turned and beat them all again, and then casually popped the ball into the net. The magic remains, and the fun and laughter generating from a lovely man. ... His record for Chelsea of forty-one First Division goals in the 1960–61 season remains a worthy monument to an unsurpassed marksman.

8

What's up, Doc?

Chelsea might have stayed in the Second Division during the 1960s but for the appointment as team manager of Tommy Docherty, the gregarious Scot with the rugged jaw. In later years after he left Stamford Bridge, Docherty was a subject for constant newspaper headlines as he sprung from manager's chair to manager's chair, the biggest explosion of all being heard when he was sacked from Manchester United in the late 1970s.

But the Chelsea job, which he took over from Ted Drake in January 1962 was the first carpenter's shop opened by the former Scotland (twenty-five caps), Celtic, Preston and Arsenal wing-half, and in the opening stages after Chelsea were promoted to the First Division in 1963 after one season away, his dovetails were slinky and smoothly interlocked. When he first took over at Stamford Bridge, Chelsea were already doomed to relegation with a team that was either too old or too young and inexperienced. Training was a bit of a joke, consisting of a few gentle laps round the greyhound track before lunch. Docherty, with his tough, absolute idealism, viewed this with horror. He introduced a thorough training programme, sold players who resented the new methods, and fined internationals for being late for training.

By the 1962-63 season, Chelsea were alive again – the ghost of the departed Jimmy Greaves had been laid, as other strikers like Barry Bridges and Bobby Tambling (future England internationals), and Bert Murray, who had all graduated from the Stamford Bridge youth nursery, began to pop in regular goals. Chelsea looked as if they were going to run away

Various forms of emotion displayed by the author (*second from left*), and friends James Michie, Karl Miller and Tony White as Chelsea miss a goal from half a yard out against West Ham ... Stamford Bridge, 1961.

with the Second Division championship at the end of 1962 but a deplorable winter, one of the worst of the century, which subsequently turned Stamford Bridge into an icicle parlour, disrupted Chelsea's consistency. The 'Doc' raged and fretted as the team began to slip back in the promotion stakes, and Chelsea masochists primed themselves – they had seen it happen before, this urge to let the treasure elude them when it was literally in their hands.

But Docherty hadn't seen it before, and when he forelornly acknowledged a seemingly crucial loss at Stamford Bridge to Stoke City, inspired by that old shuffler himself, Sir Stanley Matthews (by now in his forty-ninth year), Chelsea looked set to spend another wearisome year away from the seniors. Stoke City's win was a ticket for their own promotion – now Chelsea with two matches remaining against Sunderland and Portsmouth needed to win both to make sure of going up.

Chelsea fans bit worn finger-nails, the suspense was unyielding. The match which would almost certainly decide it all would be at Roker Park, where a mere point in front of a partisan sixty-two thousand Wearside crowd would be sufficient to give Sunderland the other promotion place. As Docherty revealed in his memoirs, it was not a time for making friends: 'At the midnight-hour, I cold-bloodedly planned the execution of Sunderland. I made the gamble of my life, and once I had mentally named the forwards I stuck to the decision. I dropped Moore, Bridges and Murray, and brought back the two toughest players in the side, Derek Kevan and Frank Upton, plus Frank Blunstone – I crossed him over to the right wing – and Bobby Tambling. And the last of the five turned out to be a master stroke. I put in wee Tommy Harmer (old swivel-hips of Spurs fame), the man I bought at the age of thirty-four to nurse and jolly my very young players along. This would be only his fifth League game of the season, but he had the ball skill to hold on and keep the line together. Looking back,' Docherty mused, 'I feel ashamed of the way I asked some of my men to play that day. Instead of being cheered off for a gallant 1–0 win, the Chelsea team were booed off. I told Kevan and Upton to harry Sunderland's Charlie Hurley unmercifully, and manfully they carried out the task.

'From the kick-off Upton raced across from his centre-forward position and aimed a wild, hard, tackle at Hurley, who had the ball. Poor Charlie went white. He wasn't used to this type of game. And from then on, wherever the ball was, one or more of my men ruthlessly hunted it.

And the goal we wanted so desperately came just before half-time when Harmer, the smallest and most inoffensive man on the field in a tough man's game, knocked in Tambling's corner with his jock-strap. In the dressing-room afterwards he walked round showing the spot from which the ball had rebounded, and calling himself Tummy Harmer.

'There was one last heart-stopping second before I knew we had won. Thousands making their way to the exits in disappointed silence halted as those who were left rekindled the Roker Roar. For the first time in the match, which was stretched into four minutes of injury time because of referee or trainer interruptions, Sunderland's left-winger Mulhall had beaten the peerless Ken Shellito. Mulhall ran into the penalty area and hit a tremendous shot just inside the near post. A goal for Sunderland then would have won them promotion by a split second. But the hurtling figure of Peter Bonetti somehow scooped the ball away, and almost immediately the upflung arms of the Chelsea team told the despondent Sunderland fans the result.'

Now there was only one match to go – at Stamford Bridge, against Portsmouth – but on a cool, clear Tuesday evening the match proved an anti-climax after Saturday's memorable rough-house. Portsmouth capitulated from the moment Kevan headed a goal for Chelsea in the second minute. And Chelsea, amid increasing enthusiasm and back-slapping, went on to win 7-0, four of them from Tambling, making his season's total thirty-nine. 'As somebody remarked in the excited hubbub afterwards,' Docherty recalled, 'Chelsea never do anything the easy way. The win at Sunderland which made promotion possible brought the first away points Chelsea had gained since Boxing Day five months earlier. My luck had certainly changed that weekend.'

In the euphoria of victory, Harry Medhurst, the Chelsea trainer and former custodian, was full of praise for the new manager: 'Tommy Docherty was unpopular when he first arrived at Stamford Bridge because he brought iron-hard discipline to the club. Now we would follow him to the end of the earth. He has won our respect.'

So Chelsea were back in the First Division, by virtue of a sneaker off their oldest player's testicles, and more than a bit of undignified hacking at the eleventh hour. Docherty now gambled on a young side (average age twenty-one) to test the seniors, ruthlessly discarding older signings like the brooding Kevan, once a regular England centre-forward. This was Tommy all over: 'In the end Kevan played only seven games for me, and as I sold him to Manchester City for £35,000 those seven games worked out at roughly £1,428 each, plus his wages, removal fees, and all the other expenses involved in a big transfer. Derek and I never saw eye to eye at all. I thought him below condition and overweight. He thought I was a cross between a sergeant-major in the glasshouse and something from the Spanish Inquisition.'

Those left behind at Stamford Bridge, the younger ones, buckled down to Docherty's intense training methods, and all seemed to work well, until on one uproarious night in 1965 Docherty sent home eight of his young squad after a night of high jinx on the town at Blackpool. This was the start of the break-up of a side Docherty had assembled with positive pride and careful thought. It was a side that came to the brink of winning everything, only to be comprehensively carved up by the manager's saw. If Docherty made major mistakes, this was surely one of them.

First there was the almost love-hate relationship he had with the club skipper, Terry Venables. Although only twenty-one, Venables, as Chelsea captain, was the all-important contributor in motivating his side's attacks. But when it came to tactics talks, Venables, as a distinguished manager-to-be, openly questioned his boss's ideas. This enraged the Glaswegian – until Venables's future at Chelsea could be numbered in months rather than years.

But for the time being, Venables was the star, the young future king of English football, the classic footballer with a brain – and what he and his young Chelsea colleagues offered on their arrival in the First Division was eminently sensational. In their first season back, they finished in fifth place, and in their second (1964–65) they had a go at winning the Treble – First Division Championship, FA Cup and Football League Cup.

It was worth being a Chelsea supporter for much of that season – there was a sense of attacking gaiety about the side, goals were plentiful, results positive, the masochists wavered as Chelsea won and won, until, in their manager's words, 'everything we had strived for went tumbling to the ground'.

First, consider the side, so young, yet so flamboyant and mature while skimping down empty lanes towards goal. Docherty had chosen well and had not had to spend a fortune in its selection – 'I had a great goal-keeper. Don't be daft, he was the best in the world, Peter Bonetti, known as the Cat in the dressing-room. He didn't have to study angles, the

Bobby Tambling, Chelsea's record aggregate goal-scorer with 202 first-team goals.

Four Chelsea managers pictured briefly smiling in one boat. *Left to right:* Docherty, McCreadie, Shellito and Sexton. Docherty was the manager at the time.

Joe Mears, Chelsea FC Chairman 1940–66.

most important knowledge a goalkeeper must have. He knew them instinctively.'

Bonetti, undoubtedly Chelsea's finest goalkeeper in their history, had been signed by the club after his mother wrote to Ted Drake from Worthing suggesting he gave the boy a trial. Bonetti made his début for Chelsea in 1960 against Manchester City and became an automatic selection for the club for thirteen seasons. In November 1973, he celebrated being the first Chelsea player to complete six hundred games – he was, overall, an astonishingly agile goalkeeper and it is a pity that the stigma of his mistakes for England against West Germany in Mexico in 1970, which cost us a place in the World Cup semi-finals, tend to obscure the overall brilliance the Cat was capable of.

In front of Bonetti, Docherty had a young exciting, all-round team: 'My back division was first class. Eddie McCreadie (twenty-four) was the best young Scot in the business; Ken Shellito, the same age, big, powerful, fearless and a ready foil to McCreadie. Both were capped for their countries. In reserve were Allan Harris (twenty-one) and his brother Ron (nineteen), who could play anywhere, and Marvin Hinton, the dual purpose player I had coveted from Charlton. When I said that he was as good a full-back as a centre-half, he proved me right when Shellito went down with cartilage trouble (an injury which would sadly end this exceptional player's career) and played out the season at right back. Similarly the cover for him, John Mortimore – at twenty-nine the senior professional – came in nobly when Hinton had to drop back from centre-half. The thought of my wing-halves brought an old-fashioned glow to my heart. Ronnie Harris was to play in every match (the man later nicknamed 'Chopper') and John Hollins (eighteen) was to miss only one. There was the even younger John Boyle at seventeen bursting to get in the side on a full-time basis.

'The forwards looked good to me. The goal machine Bobby Tambling was soon to beat the club scoring record. Venables one of the most talented readers of the game, and still only twenty-one, the flying Barry Bridges and the thoughtful Bert Murray. But although I had a number of fine young players in reserve, my own weakness was that I had no one capable of climbing high in the goalmouth.... When George Graham, not yet twenty, was put on the Aston Villa transfer list, I moved in and paid the unbelievably low figure of five thousand pounds. I couldn't believe it, even when Graham reported for training at Stamford Bridge.'

Nor could the Stamford Bridge crowd as the gifted Graham, who later won honours in Arsenal's double side, began to link astutely with Venables. For a long time, Chelsea prospered – and it did look as if they could claim the Treble – but there were booby traps carefully laid, devastating ones in fact.

On 13 March, Chelsea, despite their formidable defensive record – only one defeat in twenty games – subsided at Old Trafford by four goals to the eventual champions. To say Manchester United were stunning is an understatement – they murdered Chelsea after a mistake by McCreadie allowed George Best to score after four minutes. Herd scored two more, and Law another, as Best turned McCreadie into a loose ball of wool. Shattered by nerves before the match, the young Chelsea team sat limply on their dressing-room seats afterwards, like dunces.

If that wasn't bad enough, Chelsea supporters anticipating Wembley for the first time had to nurse devastating hangovers after Liverpool beat their nervous side in the semi-final at Villa Park. Again nerves were the problem – the Chelsea players were literally shaking before the kick-off, and although Liverpool, having just won a thrice played European Cup tie against Cologne by the toss of a coin, had been expected to be easy opponents, it did not prove to be the case. Chelsea, after having a perfectly good goal by Mortimore ruled out, were cruelly put to the sword. A brief consolation came when Chelsea won the Football League Cup in a two-leg affair against Leicester, McCreadie scoring a fabulous solo goal in the first game at home. Chelsea had won something at least, but the League effort went thoroughly to pot – and led to the eruption at Blackpool. The Chelsea kids still had a lot to learn.

Docherty had experienced his first major turbulence on this trip, sending home eight players for breaking a team curfew. The manager must have been relieved to take the side off for a sunny tour of Australia, and it was there that a major compensation was found for 'a few bittersweet memories' experienced at the end of the season.

It was in the land of the kangaroo that Docherty discovered he had a potential scoring genius in Peter Osgood, one day to be crowned 'King of Stamford Bridge'. Osgood, a talented reserve scorer in the Football Combination had been taken along for the ride because Barry Bridges was away with Sir Alf Ramsey's England squad. While Bridges scored the winning goal for England in Yugoslavia, the tall, wonderfully balanced replacement took his opportunity with evident zest. In one

match he scored six goals and hit the bar on four occasions, provoking
cheeky quips of the kind he would indulge in later: 'Sorry about the
missed ones, Boss,' he told Docherty. 'I haven't had ten since I was at
school.'

Bridges must have been pleased with his performance on the England
tour, especially as the World Cup finals were only a year away, but he
was soon to discover that the higher you get, the farther you fall. Now
he had a rival for the Chelsea No. 9 shirt – one Peter Osgood. The
manager was obviously enthralled by his new discovery's all-round
talents. 'Cliff Bastin, Tom Lawton, Stanley Matthews, Tom Finney,
Johnny Haynes, Jimmy Greaves, Alick Jeffrey, Jimmy Mullen, a few
more; they all had something which stamped them apart, that elusive
stardust which heralds greatness to come. That is what I saw in the
beanpole Osgood from the first moment I saw his casually deceptive
amble across a football field, that sinuous shift which took him past an
opponent who, left with a baffled look on his face, turned to gaze almost
in awe.... On the team-sheet I put down Osgood, 9, and the rest round
him.'

The 1965–66 season should have cemented Docherty's claim to join
that esteemed club of great managers from Chapman to Busby and
Shankly ... but like a tiger reaching the outskirts of a jungle for the kill,
they slunk back into the undergrowth eventually without even a mangy
chicken as a prize. It was a tragedy, and one for which the manager
should take a large measure of the blame. But how different it all had
seemed in the early months. Chelsea were a splendid side, and the fans
poured along the Fulham Road to cheer Terry Venables and the lads
eating up the opposition.

Chelsea did away with that sprawling slug of terracing to open a new,
all-seater West stand – although it was by no means as ambitious and
ruinously costly as the one built in the 1970s on the other side of the
ground. Increased attendances were needed to pay for the new construction, and Chelsea, much to their satisfaction, soon paid off the bill as they
reached the FA Cup semi-final, the Fairs Cup semi-final, and made a bold
challenge for the League title. Attendances at Chelsea were reduced, but
increased receipts had a healthy effect on the club's bank balance: after
the new stand was launched, Chelsea took £21,896, £20,832 and
£20,006 respectively for the Fairs Cup matches against AC Milan, TSV
Munich and Barcelona.

Chelsea were now a glamour club, there was special zing about the peanuts fresh roasted, an expectant hum when the team trotted on to the pitch – sleek, young and booming with fitness and ambition. This was the side which beat the redoubtable Manchester United after they had returned from thrashing Benfica in the European Cup in Lisbon, 'El Beatle' Best doing it almost on his own. Within four minutes Chelsea had scored two killer goals through Tambling and Graham – the sixty thousand crowd yelling themselves into a frenzy – and Best, as an anti-climax, found himself tackled out of the game by Joe Kirkup, whom Docherty had just signed from West Ham.

It was players like Best, Law and Charlton, and the Chelsea kids who helped turn soccer in England into something eminently trendy – with England's World Cup victory against West Germany only months away. A large new group of fans started going along to watch Saturday's match at Stamford Bridge, and down the Fulham Road to Craven Cottage; various showbiz and other glossy customers emerged wearing fur and leather and with tiny cheeroots pressed between refined thumb and forefinger – articulate property dealers, inaudible starlets, chauvinist actors, fledgling models, unshaven members of the rag trade, solemn artists, rural antique dealers. On match days, they dropped everything else and made for the football ground.

Stamford Bridge, and the players themselves had also changed. Jimmy Hill had done his thorough work for the Players Union in having the restrictive maximum wage rule abolished in 1961, and the players, on rapidly escalating wages and bonus systems, played their part like leading young executives; older Chelsea footballers who had trudged from the Tube to play at Stamford Bridge gave forth pained smiles at the news that Johnny Haynes of Fulham had become the first £100 a week footballer – *they* hadn't. By the 1980s, players thought nothing of asking for one thousand pounds a week. As Albert Stubbins, the former Liverpool centre-forward, said somewhat ruefully recently: 'How different from the days when stars wore baggy shorts and big leather boots. In those days they tended to holiday at Blackpool, Bournemouth, Torquay and Scarborough, and drink pints with soccer supporters in working men's clubs.'

The old-fashioned image had left Stamford Bridge, the cloth caps and duffle coats had gone with the 1950s – the young men of Chelsea were living well off the pitch, and playing like a dream on it. In a play-off against AC Milan in Italy in the Fairs Cup, they won so handsomely that Bernard Joy in the *Evening Standard* could barely restrain his pen from bursting into flames:

'Chelsea tried all the moves against Milan . . . short passes, long cross-field passes, decoy running, overlaps, individual breaks, short corners, long ones, wall passes. In those early, breath-taking minutes they overran Milan and their grim defensive scheme, and forced them to disgorge two goals, more than they had given away in any previous match that season. Venables was the showman of the match; Hinton outdid Maldini as a sweeper centre-half; the dark head of Graham was always menacing; and Ron Harris relentlessly mastered Amarildo, the Brazilian World Cup star.

'Hollins snapped like a terrier round the heels of Rivera, and his wing-half partner, Boyle, put so much concentration and guts into the game that he had a reaction of stomach upset and was sent home afterwards. Osgood produced the moment of sheer magic when he brought down a centre, dummied Maldini to one side and hit a left-foot shot which Balzarini could only watch. He showed other flashes of genius without making as much impression on the whole ninety minutes as many of his colleagues. After a few weeks below form, McCreadie played with his usual fire and assurance. . . .'

It was too good to be true – and the greatest thing of all at this time was the maturity shown by Docherty's kids. In a previous Fairs Cup game, they had survived the brutal bottle-throwing (Boyle was knocked out) by the incensed supporters of FC Roma, who had been aroused into predictable frenzy by the reports of Eddie McCreadie's sending-off at Stamford Bridge in the first leg. Such hatred continued until after the match, when the victorious Chelsea players, who had hung grimly on to a 4-1 first leg lead, made their getaway in a battered and manhandled coach.

Their maturity showed too when it came to taking on Liverpool, the Cup holders, in a third round match at Anfield. Despite their recent achievements, nobody gave Docherty's men much chance of beating Shankly's team.

But Chelsea, after being a goal behind through Roger Hunt's whizz-bang in ninety-one seconds, produced one of the finest team performances in their history, winning 2-1 with goals by Osgood and Tambling. Sensational stuff – and a sporting Liverpool chairman said to Joe Mears afterwards: 'We are due to send the Cup back to the Football Association next week. Do us a favour and take it back with you – you've earned it.'

Chelsea returned home feeling very pleased with themselves – but somewhere, peeping out of a nearby attic, was a witch ready to put a curse on the club. A nearly great team was about to break up, their manager reacting like a child knocking over a pile of bricks. Suddenly Venables, who had done so much to encourage his team, was on the transfer list – the twenty-one-year-old captain placed there by a manager who proclaimed he had endured enough 'the number of times [Venables] had cockily interrupted me during training. The rift between myself and my captain was exploded beyond repair.'

Venables had been one of the players sent home from Blackpool, and like McCreadie, who had earlier declared he would never play for the club again, he became more and more perturbed about his manager's attitude. Despite being on the list, Venables carried on playing for Chelsea, but morale had begun to sink. It was awful, Chelsea were on the skids again, losing another semi-final at Villa Park, this time against a Sheffield Wednesday team inspired by Jim McCalliog, one of Docherty's discards.

Another defeat, in the semi-final of the Fairs Cup against Barcelona, increased the rift between Docherty and some of his team. With the arrival of Charlie Cooke from Dundee United, a more portly Cooke than the slim-line version who helped Chelsea win the FA Cup four years later, Docherty decided there would be no place for Venables and the new arrival in the same team. Venables was out in the cold, soon to be transferred to Spurs, where he would perform with verve and distinction. By now the bricks were falling fast.

Bridges, who had been hurt at having to move to outside right to accommodate Osgood, was transferred to Birmingham. Murray joined him, while Graham, a marvellously fluent performer, went off to Arsenal and helped them win the Double. Chelsea reeled slightly: the League title had blown away; Everton were the new FA Cup holders; and all those sweet things created in the Fairs Cup were aborted by the harsh Catalans.

While England rejoiced that summer at the winning of the World Cup, Docherty brooded about the break-up of his team, and the new set-up to come. Cooke's transfer to Chelsea was followed by Tommy Baldwin's from Arsenal, and when Osgood unluckily broke his leg in a League Cup match early in the 1966–67 season, Docherty went out and

Three Chelsea players past and present in confrontation during the 1967 'Cockney Cup Final'. Ron Harris, Chelsea's captain, challenges Jimmy Greaves, now wearing a Spurs shirt, and lurking behind is Terry Venables, another erstwhile Chelsea favourite.

bought Tony Hateley, a goal nodder, from Aston Villa. Hateley, who had been coached by Tommy Lawton, was a fair performer in the air, but on the ground he could look like a park novice. Docherty admitted that the move obstructed rather than favoured Chelsea tactics, which were geared to running off the ball, and moving the ball quickly on the ground. Hateley galloped around, demanding high centres and generally behaving like a performer from another, distant era.

To Docherty's credit, his latest recruit did produce one memorable and outstanding goal for Chelsea in their third FA Cup semi-final in succession – again at Villa Park and this time against Leeds United. He put all his power behind a cross from Cooke and sent the ball hurtling into the net. At last, after years of trying, Chelsea were at Wembley – and yet almost not. In injury time, Lorimer sent a free kick soaring in past Bonetti, but the referee ruled that one out because he said he hadn't blown for the kick to be taken. Lucky Chelsea, but it only made up for so many misfortunes in the past.

The 1967 Cockney Cup Final between Chelsea and Spurs was only really memorable from the North London team's point of view – they played the football, and scored two killer goals through Robertson and Saul, two players briefed to play wide on Wembley's open spaces. Chelsea seemed bogged down and full of their own inertia in the sunshine, although if a startling drive by Cooke had not been saved beautifully by Jennings just before Robertson's first half goal, Chelsea might have pulled themselves together. One of the Chelsea team that day blamed his side's lethargy on eating too much chop suey: 'We got the notion Chinese food was light,' he said bitterly, 'but I was so full of flaming bean-shoots that I felt like a becalmed junk.'

Tambling did save Chelsea's pride with a late goal, but Spurs, including two former Chelsea players, Venables and Greaves, in their team, in general had very little to worry about, apart from one or two inspired pieces of dribbling by Hateley, of all people. It was almost as if a fairy godmother had suddenly ordained him Stanley Matthews. The Chelsea team at Wembley was: Bonetti, A. Harris, McCreadie, Hollins, Hinton, R. Harris, Cooke, Baldwin, Hateley, Tambling and Boyle.

The final was virtually Docherty's swansong at the Bridge. The death of chairman Joe Mears, who had an ability to get on with the fiery Scot, produced a successor, Charles Pratt, and the new Chelsea board lurched through a number of rows involving the manager and team. Docherty threatened to leave the club, and eighteen players joined in the circus demanding transfers. The row had essentially been over the distribution of Cup tickets – but the overall mood at Chelsea harboured discontent. A bad start to the 1967–68 season, including a 6–2 home defeat by Southampton, helped matters not at all, and that autumn, the self-confessed 'blabber-mouth' was invited to take his services elsewhere by the Chelsea board. Docherty had been at Stamford Bridge for six roller-coaster years. If anything, it had been well worth the ride.

9

Sexton's Blues Forever

Tommy Docherty's successor at Chelsea was the shy, retiring Dave Sexton, a man as different in character and personality as James Stewart's from James Cagney's on screen. Sexton came to Stamford Bridge with a sound coaching reputation built at Arsenal; he had played for West Ham with Malcolm Allison and John Bond; he had a shrewd football brain, and although an introvert, his childhood as the son of an East End boxer had given him a built-in defensive system.

Sexton eschewed bizarre transfer ideals at Chelsea, like Docherty's signing of Alex Stepney, the Millwall goalkeeper, when he already was served by the brilliant Bonetti. That kind of action was bound to cause friction, Stepney only playing one League game for Chelsea before going to Manchester United. Sexton, in contrast, searched for useful long-term investments like David Webb, a Southampton defender, bought for £60,000; John Dempsey, the Fulham and Republic of Ireland centre-back for another £60,000; and perhaps the most valuable of all, striker Ian Hutchinson from Cambridge United for a mere £5,000. And on the fringes of the first team was the seventeen-year-old Alan Hudson, a Chelsea resident brought up in a pre-fab, who had been turned down by Fulham but now showed signs of a gifted future.

Biding his time, Sexton carefully reshaped his first team, Alan Birchenall bowing out, and Alan Hudson's flair introduced in midfield; Peter Houseman was also given a regular place as a retractable left-winger. The old Docherty guard remained, including Eddie McCreadie, John Hollins, Ron Harris, Charlie Cooke and Peter Osgood; but Bobby Tambling, a true Chelsea servant, moved on to Crystal Palace.

Tambling, who became a Jehovah's Witness, eventually moved to Ireland to play out his footballing career – but he had left a formidable legacy behind at Stamford Bridge as the club's record aggregate scorer with 202 goals. It was difficult getting used to no longer seeing Bobby swoop downfield at the Bridge, head thrust forward, legs pumping the turf, an almost boyish flush tinting his cheeks. And then that explosive shot that would tingle the fingers of goalkeepers, or those carefully laid back low centres ready for killing.

Now the scene moved conveniently to the fluttering feet of Charlie Cooke. In his early days at Chelsea, he had suffered from weight problems, not to mention a certain reluctance to go along with club rules about dieting. Cooke liked nothing more in his spare time than to sit up late chatting to influential people about literature, Scott Fitzgerald, and the shape of the modern novel. His form on the football field varied considerably. He was capable in one game of murdering the opposition, while in another he would disappear from the game, lost in his own private world.

It was not until the 1969–70 season that Cooke's career really bloomed – like a reluctant rose. With Osgood and Hutchinson putting the ball regularly into the net, Cooke made it his duty to get the ball to them; it was a task of total commitment, a consistent one at last, and, ultimately, a deadly one. The boy who had once spent hours kicking a tennis ball against a street wall in Aberdeen, now dodged, sprinted, loped, accelerated, twisted, weaved in, weaved out, jinked forward, fluttered out, sprung in, floated over ... the ball was his to command. And with Hudson shaping his own beautiful talents alongside, Chelsea made their way once again to Wembley.

In documenting those exciting times, mention must be made of the football era involved, not a very appetizing one in many aspects. After England's World Cup win in 1966, League clubs had rushed like the famous herd of swine to cast out wingers. Sir Alf Ramsey's doctrines had become sacred, and eventually, for the poor football fan, negative and boring. It was the era of Storey and Hunter, of escalating hooliganism, of kick and kick back both on and off the pitch; and it was an era of change, with substitutes allowed in League matches for the first time.

Away from the unsavoury aspects of those times, Sexton modelled a team which, although hardly saintly when it came to mixing it, was capable of playing effervescent football, and scoring goals which were dramatic and tingling in the memory. Two at least deserve mention, First

At Old Trafford in December 1969, Charlie Cooke hits a fierce shot that Manchester United's goalkeeper Alex Stepney can only deflect – for Hutchinson to score.

Cooke is a guest at the Football Writers' Dinner at the Café Royal, 1970.

Division goals at their best, both scored in 1970, Chelsea's Cup-winning year. The first by Hudson against Sheffield Wednesday in March was reminiscent of Jimmy Greaves at his most devastating: a long, elusive dribble from just inside his own half, past four men, and the final shot planted with pinpoint accuracy. The second, in August against Arsenal, was inspired by the energies of Hollins, a player who must have run more for Chelsea during his span there than any other wearer of blue in the club's history. The goal followed Hollins's solo dash to reach a through ball by Ron Harris. Although the speed of his run was almost frantic, Hollins managed to hold off Roberts's challenge, swerve left and chip the ball over Bob Wilson's head. A steaming 53,722 crowd at Stamford Bridge were on the brink of applauding Chelsea's winning goal when the ball came back from the crossbar. That might have been it, but Hollins summoned up colossal energy to reach the ball again ahead of the Arsenal defence and drove the ball right-footed into the roof of the net. You could have heard the crowd cheering that one at Hyde Park Corner.

Not surprisingly Chelsea put themselves in line to win something. By the spring of 1970, Sexton's legion were marching confidently on the paved road towards Wembley – the flower seller down the Kings Road offered his view of the future free of charge: 'I think, Ossie and the lads have got a real chance this year, honest, I do – they've got that stamp of the excellent, you see. Ossie for Wembley, be sure!'

At Loftus Road on a mudpatch, Chelsea revealed all their strengths in the sixth round against Queen's Park Rangers. There was a new gate record of 33,572 watching the match, and with the Second Division side fielding such entertaining players as Rodney Marsh, and Chelsea's former warrior, Terry Venables, it looked like being a merry party – and it was. Chelsea's 4-2 victory was achieved with a combination of skill and heavy traction work on the muddy surface, the opening goal made and finished off by Dave Webb with the kind of opportunism that would reward this gifted defender in the final replay. Three more goals by Peter Osgood, plus his fourth booking of the season, unhinged Queen's Park Rangers, but if anything showed up in the game it was the strengths of Chelsea's midfield, and the chloroformic effect of 'Chopper' Harris's tackling against the normally insidious Marsh. A *Sunday Telegraph* correspondent wrote in his report of the game: 'As expected, Chelsea's superior skills, talents and assiduous teamwork, in which Houseman, the remarkable

Hudson, Hollins and Osgood flamboyantly excelled, outpowered and destroyed all the Trojan work that Rangers put into this oven of a quarter-final. . . . How bravely the Rangers team fought but up front this was not Marsh's day by courtesy of Ron Harris, who played him so closely that their respective numbers often turned from 6 and 10 into 610. . . .'

The semi-final at Tottenham against Third Division Watford, who had surprisingly knocked out Liverpool in the previous round, provided few complications for Chelsea once an early precocious challenge had been overruled. The final score was 5–1 – and Chelsea were at Wembley again. The opposition were at first not readily known – Leeds United and Manchester United locked in one of those duels of heavy bombardments that devastate the earth but provide little sign of creating a breakthrough. Eventually Leeds made a hole in the wire and prepared to face Chelsea for the Cup.

The teams came to Wembley on a sunny April afternoon with enough talent on both sides to fry up a classic. Jack Charlton, Norman Hunter and Allan Clarke, and Chelsea's Peter Osgood and Peter Bonetti were all listed members of Alf Ramsey's ill-fated Mexican World Cup expedition for the weeks ahead; while the fiery Billy Bremner, as a travelling spectator down Mexico way, would enjoy his ice-cold gin and tonics, if nothing else. But first things first: Leeds, who had been tumbling of late at the last fence, were desperate to get their hands on the FA Cup – it was the season for them to win it; they looked strong, they played hard, they ran hard; they were Don Revie's New Model Army hell bent on knocking the Southern sissies out of Wembley.

Chelsea had suffered an impediment a week or two earlier, when Hudson was hit by ligament trouble, and had a leg put in plaster. No magical final then for the boy wonder – his fingers-crossed pose for the photographers during Wembley week suggested optimism, but it was a hopeless case. Chelsea now had to rearrange their team, and it was Baldwin, a recent substitute, who got Sexton's nod of approval.

The sports writers hardly agreed about the outcome. There was a heavy lobby in favour of Revie's team, a more mature, balanced, experienced side, but others like Geoffrey Green of *The Times* had a sneaking feeling that the old victims of music hall clowns would spring a surprise. Charlie Cooke, a guest a few days before at the Football Writers dinner, was confident about Chelsea's chances: 'We'll have to cash in on their mistakes – they're bound to make the odd vital one. We'll come down on them, make them pay.'

The teams at Wembley on 11 April 1970 were:

Chelsea: Bonetti, Webb, McCreadie, Hollins, Dempsey, R. Harris (sub Hinton), Baldwin, Houseman, Osgood, Hutchinson, Cooke.

Leeds United: Sprake, Madeley, Cooper, Bremner, Charlton, Hunter, Lorimer, Clarke, Jones, Giles, Gray.

Referee: E. Jennings (Stourbridge).

Wheep – Mr Jennings blew, and they were away on a shocking pitch, full of ruts and hollows, bits of straw, lumpy mud, and areas of soggy no-go. Surely this was not Wembley, the golden pitch trodden so dramatically by Stanley Matthews when he beat Bolton Wanderers wearing bedroom slippers in 1953? Now the pitch was abysmal, ruined temporarily by recent horsey events held on its illustrious turf. Even Princess Margaret, who is not adverse to watching horses perform at Badminton and Ascot, gave the toiling players of Chelsea and Leeds a sympathetic nod or two from the Royal Box as the ball flagrantly refused to rise from the morass.

Chelsea suffered first as both sides were still in a process of sorting out the reluctant leather. Geoffrey Green wrote: 'Drama was in the wind from the start. The first open hint came after twenty minutes when Charlton got above Bonetti and the rooftops to head Gray's corner. Harris and McCreadie stood guard on the Chelsea line and McCreadie should have cleared easily. But the ball, instead of bouncing, squatted like a wet sponge to slip under his foot and creep home almost apologetically.'

One–nil to Leeds, and the confidence which had taken them in earlier months towards an abortive attempt at the Grand Slam (League, Cup and European Cup) began to crackle – suddenly Leeds like white swans winged forward across an ox-bow lake; they pounced, they ran menacingly, Bremner and Giles pecking the Chelsea defence for every available opening. And the greatest sufferer from Chelsea's point of view was Dave Webb – Eddie Gray was in a weaving and unweaving mood, and the pitifully exposed Chelsea right-back was turned into a bale of wool, mocked by a 'teenage' cat. Leeds had nothing to worry about now – Gray looked on for a hat-trick.

Half-time was only a matter of minutes away, with the blessed relief of hot tea for the sufferers on the pitch, when the tall frame of Hutchinson rose, sideboards bristling, to knock sideways a cross – a chancy effort that might have meant nothing at all. But in this case the receiver, Houseman, loitering out at the angle of goal, but surely too far to do damage to Leeds, struck a not too devastating shot at Sprake's goal. No danger here, the Welsh international had it well covered, programmes were put away, eyes hovered towards the stadium exits, beer bars and tea urns. But Sprake, what was he doing, fumbling with the ball there? Suddenly the wretched object had wiggled away from his hands and plonked into the corner of the net. Sprake lay on the ground looking as if the gods should come along and order him for dinner. 1–1.

The second half was not one for those with soft limbs. The conditions sapped more and more energy, but it was Gray again who did the most damage, and but for Bonetti's twists and turns on his goal-line, Leeds must have established an irrevocable lead. But the Blues kept going, they stuck to their duties – even Webb, turned and turned by the onrushing Eddie Gray. Seven minutes from the end of full time, Leeds at last scored the goal that seemed to wrap up matters: a header by Clarke hit the post, and from the rebound, Jones struck savagely past Bonetti from an angle. Jones danced back to the halfway line to be met by his almost frantic manager, Don Revie, who hugged Jones before being almost frog-marched back to his seat by two indignant policemen.

That was it then, Chelsea had lost ... not a bad effort, but their resources hadn't been quite as efficient as Leeds, the best team had won. Well, almost!

Green was there noting Chelsea's amazing come-back with his pen: 'Yet within moments there was Hutchinson to plant a flying header past Sprake's right hand as Hollins chipped a free kick from the left to the near post. It was a well-rehearsed tactic that caught Leeds flatfooted at the last breath, their concentration perhaps already deflected by the thoughts of impending celebration. Yet if Leeds commanded much of the play, Chelsea, fired by Cooke's clever dribbling as the match wore on, showed an undying spirit, that kept them alive. Few sides come from behind twice against Leeds.'

Extra time was an anti-climax, both sides worn out by previously released energies. Chelsea came close enough to winning with a long-range dipper by Dempsey, but so did Leeds with a Clarke shot that hit the crossbar at the other end, and a rap by Giles which Webb, redeeming past failures, somehow managed to block on the line. Enough was enough

Wembley ... 11 April 1970.

Leeds open the score at Wembley through Jack Charlton's header. The ball
fails to bounce and squeezes through the legs of an abashed Eddie McCreadie.

Tommy Baldwin throws up his arms to welcome Peter Houseman's freak long-range shot which wiggled past Gary Sprake to give a first-half equalizer.

Following Mick Jones's late second goal for Leeds, Ian Hutchinson beats Sprake to make the score 2–2 with four minutes of normal time left. Dave Webb (2) and Tommy Baldwin (7) hail the effort. The game ended 2–2 after extra time.

– the referee called a halt, and it was replay time for the first time in a Wembley Cup Final. The venue chosen was Old Trafford, Manchester, eighteen days later.

After Chelsea's trainer, Harry Medhurst, who would have made a Cup Final appearance himself for the club in 1950 but for that piece of impertinence by Arsenal's Freddie Cox, had done his work on strained muscles with a busy bunch of gnarled fingers, the Stamford Bridge lads made their way north for another session on the Leeds treadmill. Manager Sexton made a sound tactical change with Ron Harris taking over the right-back spot from the unhappy Webb, who moved into the centre of the defence. On the Leeds side, Sprake, still suffering nightmares from his Wembley boob, and now injured too, made way for the twenty-three-year-old Harvey. Again, the early stages of the match saw Chelsea outplayed and outrun, Jones looking particularly dangerous with his lone patrols. As Green recalled: 'This was no match for weaklings. As the sun dipped out of sight over Old Trafford's mighty stands, it seemed to take with it flaming streamers of the day; and it left behind a bonfire. Here was a match of gleaming steel, mostly with the broadsword, which was used with impunity by both sides and allowed to be used by a referee (Mr Jennings) who would have a short life in Latin America.'

Tumble, tumble, rage, rage, 'Take his name, ref' – 'Show us your loser's medals,' – 'bite his legs, Norm' – 'the bonfire' burned brightly ... and then, almost imperceptibly, Leeds scored – with Bonetti still limping after a heavy challenge from Jones. It was Jones, nine minutes before half-time, who put Leeds into the lead with a blazing cross-shot out of Bonetti's reach. The blue-and-white wall of colour behind one goal remained frozen – could Chelsea possibly come back again? It seemed doubtful. It looked more likely that Leeds, with their titanic advances, would add quickly to their lead – but the Chelsea defence held firm, Webb, in particular, erasing all the doubts about his presence in the replay after the Wembley fiasco, with some timely tackles.

The game wore on, banging and clanking, almost murderous in its exchanges. Then came a turnabout. Chelsea started playing some sweet football, Osgood, Cooke and Hollins moving the ball between them with a confidence not shown before – and Leeds began to scratch their heads. It couldn't happen again ... but it did. And Cooke was master in charge, with every Chelsea man in support. Hollins, Hutchinson, Osgood and finally Cooke exchanged passes – and when Cooke's chip came over

Ron Harris introduces Peter Osgood to Princess Margaret before the final.

29 April 1970. Peter Osgood heads his famous equalizer from Charlie Cooke's pass at Old Trafford.

And the one that really counted: Norman Hunter looks horrified as Dave Webb heads Chelsea's most memorable goal off his cheek-bone to win the FA Cup in extra time.

The aftermath.

as precise and shining as a Cartier diamond, Osgood dived in from the blind side and headed a devastating goal past Harvey.

What a pleasure it was a few weeks later during the World Cup to sit with Cooke by a Mexican swimming pool and savour that goal. 'Ossie was incredible, he made for the ball as if he wanted to knock a hole right through Manchester,' the modest Charlie said, flicking a bit of duck-blue pool water up with a bare toe.

At one-all, it was extra time, and more busy work by Harry Medhurst and the Leeds trainer on wincing limbs, and clobbered shins. Mr Jennings gave another piercing bleep, and the men at war took up their 'broad-swords' again. What happened next was to become a piece of Chelsea forklore, with Webb, the present manager of Bournemouth, the hero of an ecstatic Chelsea night.

The Leeds players had known all about the strength of Hutchinson's long throw, and throughout the gruelling marathon of two games had kept their binoculars firmly on any approaching missiles thrown by the tall striker. Seconds before the end of the extra-time interval, however, they were caught in a tizzy by one such long throw from the left and when Charlton, challenged by Osgood, misdirected his header across goal, Webb powered in and headed the ball just inside the angle. Bedlam! Webb was nearly hurled to the ground by his overjoyed teammates. It was now Leeds's turn to be trailing, and with Hinton brought on for Osgood, to add to Chelsea's defensive wall, they finally failed, McCreadie once kicking off the line during a ten-man Leeds attack. Mr Jennings pressed a hand firmly on his whistle and blew. Blue was very definitely the colour.

All kinds of flickering images were collected from this marvellous finale for Chelsea and the jovial Webb – his gigantic leap to score, his even higher victory leap afterwards, Hunter sitting on the ground looking horrified, Charlton looking thunderous, Chelsea fans at Old Trafford or back home in front of the television, going berserk with their blue-and-white scarves, biting the ears off the blue-and-white teddy bears, pressing sweaty fingers in each other's eyes, and yelling 'Webb, we love you' and 'Sexton, you're marvellous,' throwing ashtrays, kissing.

Meanwhile, Geoffrey Green had picked up his pen in the Old Trafford Press Box and was writing Leeds's obituary.... 'Looking back on the long struggle, we can now say that Chelsea came three times from behind to match the League champions of last year and finally snatched the

The goal-scorers kiss the cup.

Dave Webb celebrates.

Cartoon by Nicholas Garland.

Post-victory celebrations.

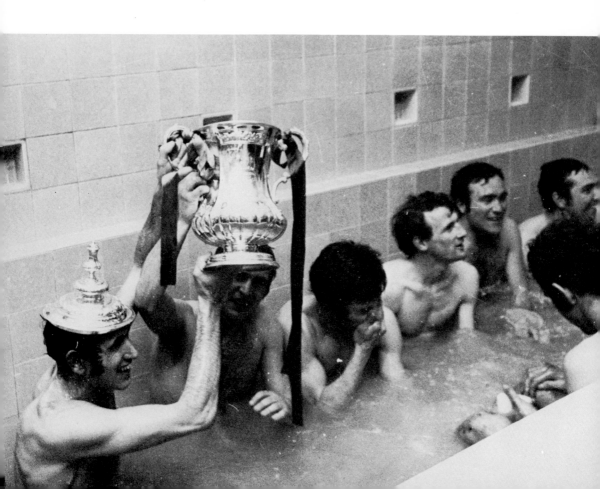

winner fifteen minutes in the extra period. Any side that can do that against such a worthy foe from Yorkshire deserve their trophy. So, with an historic touch about it, Chelsea have at last won the prize which they first played for at Old Trafford in the final of 1915.... Leeds, like Sisyphus, have pushed three boulders to the top of three mountains and are now left to see them all back in the dark of the valley....'

Television commentator Brian Moore wasn't the only one to lose his voice – yells of joy in the Chelsea dressing-room after Ron Harris had been presented with the FA Cup thundered out of the steam into a Mancurian night sky; a benign Brian Mears and Lord Chelsea dispensed champagne, and there was a feeling of raucous madness caused by victory. Leeds couldn't take it – they refused to collect their losers' medals, they sulked, they muttered, they stooped as if the world was against them. If only someone could have told them they would be back to win an FA Cup Final in two years' time. Failure clings like spilt syrup.

The celebrations in Manchester and down in Chelsea had reached fever pitch. A lone Pensioner, enjoying his normal ration of Guinness, was passed round the saloon bar in the arms of screaming fans. Klaxons blared along the Kings and Fulham Roads, landlords offered free drinks, and Dave Webb summed up his triumph with a grin that stretched from Manchester Piccadilly to Fulham Broadway: 'At Wembley, I was the whipping boy, getting that terrible run around from Eddie Gray. Shattered me, he did. The more I thought about it, the worse I felt. But Dave Sexton built me right up again for the replay. As soon as that first game was over, we knew we'd got to change the defence. Dave said Ron Harris would tight mark Gray, and I was to take Allan Clarke. Perhaps we'd have played it this way at Wembley if Ron had been properly fit. Anyway, the switch worked just as we had hoped. Ron did a great job against Gray, and besides watching Clarke, I had scope to have a go up front.

'But at half-time, when I looked at Peter Bonetti's left knee and saw it had ballooned right up, I was afraid they'd be sticking me in goal for the second half. I told Harry Medhurst, "Do a good job on him, mate – he looks better in the green jersey than I do."

'I knew once Ossie got that first goal we could do it. We've every sympathy for Leeds, who were in with a chance of three big prizes a few weeks ago. Through the season we've admired them. Now we've beaten the favourites. It's unbelievable.'

So Chelsea prepared to move back south after the end of their most remarkable and productive season – FA Cup holders for the first time, and proud occupants of third place in Division I. The scenes on their arrival to join a victory bus at Euston are remembered by Frank Keating, then an ITV sports producer:

'ITV had put a fee into Eddie McCreadie's players' pool to cover the triumphant coach-run exclusively. So we had a shock at Euston when the police refused to allow me and our cameraman on board. We pleaded with them, but they refused, and the victory bus drove off without us. We decided to give chase, my colleague lugging his camera along with him. You could hear Ossie and the boys singing their heads off. Then the bus stopped at a traffic light and we caught up. Nobody stopped us getting on this time and we had a whale of a time for the rest of the journey.

'Ossie was mine host, and I remember Dave Sexton sitting quietly in a corner downstairs saying nothing and hardly believing Chelsea had really won the Cup. Most of the boys were on the open deck upstairs and when we hit the Fulham Road, the crowds went barmy, waving and singing. The welcome-home reception was held at Fulham Town Hall because Hammersmith Council had put in their claim before Kensington and Chelsea, who wanted the show to go on at Chelsea Town Hall. The players weren't worried – they could have held it in the buffet of Euston Station for all they cared – they were floating up in the blue, blue sky. Brian Mears had a permanent grin on his face. Honestly, mate, it *was* a lovely day to be at Stamford Bridge.'

In Chelsea it was like Armistice, VE and Coronation nights rolled into one – those who remembered Chelsea with affection from the old music hall days linked arms with younger ones, who could just recall dad raving about Roy Bentley. Every little side street from the World's End to Fulham Broadway had a private party; 'Knees Up, Mother Webbie', 'Nice one', 'Get you', 'On the moon last year, over the moon this year', 'Come on, Ossie, sing us a song', 'There's a Silver Lining', 'Chelsea in the Sky with Diamonds', 'Charlie, I wanna hold your hand', 'Blue Moon, beside you I kneel and pray', 'Come on, you BLUES', 'Mum, give us another', 'Harris is a butcher, a loverly butcher.'

'Darlings, wasn't that fantastic,' Dickie Attenborough yodelled in more sophisticated places, actor friends ready to raise a jar of champers. Dickie, Chelsea director, distinguished actor, hero of *The Angry Silence*,

The Cup Winners return home . . . Fulham Road, 30 April.

Brian Mears, Chelsea's Chairman, proudly displays the FA Cup he spent the night with.

Chelsea FC, FA Cup Winners, 1970.

FA Charity Shield 1970. A bearded Dave Webb challenges Everton's Alan
Ball at Stamford Bridge. Everton won 2–1.

On the prowl . . . manager Dave Sexton leads off on a training session with Dave Webb supporting (*second from right*).

was hardly reticent now – his smile lit up the towpaths of his homeland, Richmond, where the Mears family had once run cut-price coaches for local fans to Stamford Bridge. The showbusiness world rejoiced – Michael Crawford and Terry Stamp walked tall. Had it really happened? Yes it had – Chelsea had won the Cup!

10

Ecstasy and Agony

I Good Years

The celebrations went on as far as a jubilant Chelsea side were concerned for at least another year when the club won their first non-domestic trophy, the European Cup Winners Cup. But by then, Sexton had introduced new faces into the side, and, despite the exciting victory at the second attempt over an ageing Real Madrid side in Athens, some of the initial impact and spontaneous flair began to dull.

At the start of the 1970-71 season, Chelsea proudly paraded a new winger, Keith Weller from Millwall. Sturdy, speedy, gifted, with a fair old shot, Weller was the man Sexton hoped would do for Chelsea what Jairzinho had done recently for Brazil in Mexico. Blow Sir Alf, wingers were back in fashion. On the way back from watching the World Cup, Sexton had been so excited at the prospect of signing Weller that he reluctantly declined an invitation from a friend to stop off in New York to hear some modern jazz – a great sacrifice by a Thelonious Monk disciple.

In August, Chelsea weaved happily around the Stamford Bridge pitch, parading the FA Cup from the old greyhound track, Everton, the opposition, had a show too, before the Charity Shield match, lofting their bit of silver, the League Championship trophy. With Alan Ball rampant, Everton won the Charity Shield by beating a peculiarly sloppy Chelsea side 2-1.

Still, it wasn't at all a bad season from Chelsea's point of view, although the real London stars of the moment were Arsenal, who followed Spurs in achieving the Double. But Chelsea made the long haul to the European

Cup Winners final by beating the holders, Manchester City, in a two-leg affair. Now they flew east for a confrontation with Real Madrid in the heat of a Greek evening. Date: 19 May 1971. Venue: Karaiskaki Stadium, Athens. Teams:

Chelsea: Bonetti, Boyle, Dempsey, Webb, Harris, Hollins (sub Mulligan), Hudson, Cooke, Weller, Osgood (sub Baldwin), Houseman.

Real: Borja, Luis, Benito, Zoco, Zunzunegui, Pirri, Grosso, Velazquez, Perez (sub Fleitas), Amancio, Gento (sub Grande).

Referee: R. Scheurer (Switzerland).

Again this was a night of high tension, but unlike the dramatic finish at Old Trafford a year before, it was the Spaniards who caught Chelsea by the tail at the eleventh hour to force a replay forty-eight hours later. Not that Chelsea had really deserved to win a fascinating battle – the old heads of Amancio, Pirri, Velazquez, Zoco, and the venerable Gento, Real's mighty winger during their herculean Di Stefano and Puskas days, continuously foxed the Londoners with their artistic notions. At times, during the first half at least, it seemed as if the clock had been turned back ten or eleven years to the glorious days when the Madrid club feasted on success.

Chelsea had to run in the shadows for a long time, then out of the blue Athens sky they came up with a goal that fairly stunned the Spaniards and silenced the *Olés*. Cooke, who had done so much to calm down his sagging side, by holding the ball and keeping possession, found Boyle in open space and when the Scot's low centre came across goal, Osgood redeemed a fairly pedestrian display by hitting a left-foot shot past Borja. Cooke, for a time, took over the proceedings, running and feinting towards the Real defenders. Chelsea now camouflaged a previous death wish, they played with conviction, and the 41,000 crowd began to applaud. But Real had other ideas – and in a last-gasp finish they pounded the Chelsea goal. With seconds remaining, and Chelsea surely there, Amancio and Pirri launched a final attack. A miskick by Dempsey, and Zoco shot past Bonetti. Now there was extra time, and the Spaniards might well have won but for some epic work by Bonetti, Webb and Boyle at the rear. So on to the replay.

With two days to wait in sublime conditions, both camps pondered over the ifs and buts of the first game – Sexton bit his lower lip and

Ecstasy in Athens as Peter Osgood scores Chelsea's winning goal against Real Madrid in the European Cup Winners' Cup Final replay May 1971.

Dave Sexton (*second from right*) briefs his team for extra time in the first match.

Ron Harris holds the trophy aloft, while the bristly Dave Webb shows his
pleasure.

brooded long into a hot Greek night. Finally he decided to play a 4–2–4 formation against the Madridists with Baldwin slotting into a striking position alongside Osgood. The teams lined up thus:

Chelsea: Bonetti, Boyle, Dempsey, Webb, Harris, Cooke, Hudson, Weller, Baldwin, Osgood (sub Smethurst), Houseman.

Real: Borja, Luis, Benito, Zoco, Zunzunegui, Pirri, Grosso, Velazquez, (sub Gento), Fleitas, Amancio, Bueno (sub Grande).

Referee: A. Bucheli (Switzerland).

Sexton's revised tactics worked during the first half, when Baldwin's introduction allowed Osgood more freedom to roam and cause disorder. In seven minutes just after the first half-hour, Chelsea took a 2–0 lead, and the Spaniards were shocked by their sheer piracy. The first was a defender's goal – Dempsey hitting a stunning shot into the roof of the Madrid net after Borja's weak punch out from Houseman's corner had come neatly his way. A goal the Irishman would always remember with pride. Another Chelsea goal arrived seven minutes later, Baldwin taking a pass from Harris and clipping a through ball to Osgood. The 'King of Stamford Bridge' did a shimmy-shake and sent the ball hurtling into the Spaniards' net.

Now it was Chelsea who were masters, and Hudson, relishing this final after missing Wembley and Old Trafford a year before, came to the forefront, raising his side when they looked like flagging. Cooke again was in superb form, and Webb a constant toiler whenever Real pressed forward at Bonetti's goal. With fifteen minutes to go, Fleitas scored for Real, and in the closing minutes, Bonetti made an extraordinary save to catch a diving header by Zoco, and Webb, with a typical piece of bravery in blocking Amancio's bull-like charge on the line, saved Chelsea from another period of extra time. The Swiss referee came to the rescue, blowing his whistle – the guillotine had fallen on the Spaniards, while for Chelsea the ending must have felt like finding a distant oasis at the last gasp.

It was hard on the Spaniards after their great performance in the previous game, and heroes like Zoco, Amancio and Pirri, who played with his left wrist strapped, had nothing to be ashamed about. As for Chelsea, they deserved the explosive reception that came their way on their triumphant coach ride from Heathrow to Stamford Bridge. Times were good for Chelsea, but in the words of Bob Dylan, they were 'a-changing'.

Chelsea FC, winners of the European Cup Winners' Cup, 1971.

Another major trophy gained, Sexton pondered over his team's make-up for the next season. Without the striking power of Ian Hutchinson, who had been out of the side for some time because of a serious knee injury, he bought Chris Garland from Bristol City to try to add more thrust alongside Osgood.

Hutchinson meanwhile had to endure the frustration of missing Chelsea's winning run in Europe. When he eventually did make the team again, Bill Shankly, no less, offered testimony: 'I'm delighted to hear that Ian is playing again. He has been so desperately unlucky with injuries, and I sincerely hope he makes a complete recovery. Hutchinson is a big, brave lad who has skill as well as courage – the type of bustling striker who is a rare commodity these days. He has the longest throw-in I have seen.' Hutchinson's bravery spanned times of agony and frustration through countless injuries. Eventually he had to retire from the game before he should have done, and for a time he was a member of the Stamford Bridge backroom staff, on the promotions side. Later, 'Hutch' and 'Ossie' went into partnership as proprietors of a pub at Old Windsor that was appropriately re-named 'The Union Inn'.

Sexton had soon become disillusioned with the willing but equally disillusioned Weller, whose skills did not impress the Stamford Bridge fans. Weller moved on, as Chelsea made a bold bid to win another trophy in the 1971–72 season. This time they reached Wembley again in the final of the Football League Cup against Stoke.

Chelsea had beaten Spurs in the semi-final, and were favourites to win the trophy for the second time. They were still Sexton's blue-eyed boys; they made a best-selling record, *Blue is the Colour, Chelsea is our Name*; they peered out of advertising hoardings; Ossie was the permanent king. Some thought the side had become a trifle big-headed. It certainly appeared so at Wembley, when they fiddled and fumbled and lost 2-1, the winning goal scored by that old fox, George Eastham. Around this time, Chelsea met defeat in the FA Cup fifth round, 3-2 away to Orient, again revealing uncharacteristic defensive mistakes. A year later, with Bill Garner and Steve Kember installed, they reached the sixth round of the FA Cup, losing to Arsenal in a replay. In the first match at Stamford Bridge, Osgood had scored one of his greatest goals, but by now his time at Stamford Bridge was limited.

Chelsea had now launched their mammoth project – the two-million-pound stand which, the club forecast, would one day make

Blue is the colour . . . Chelsea is our name . . .

Stamford Bridge the finest stadium in the country. The old main stand came down, the famous George Hilsdon weather vane which, it had been said, would bring instant ill fortune to Chelsea if ever it was pulled down, was put away in some unseen shed and forgotten. Stamford Bridge, shorn of Gus Mears's solid, steel cover, as familiar as Covent Garden, now looked an eerie desert, with cranes and brooding scaffolding hanging over the pitch. The players assembled in a nearby mobile changing-room and trudged through a temporary gate to play ... it certainly affected Chelsea, their play began to creak, they lost silly matches, their confidence went, and loyal servants like Charlie Cooke were allowed to disappear to Crystal Palace for £85,000.

In November 1973 Osgood followed four previous Chelsea England internationals in scoring a hundred League goals for the club – the ton achieved with a masterly angled shot against Everton. (His predecessors were Bobby Tambling, Roy Bentley, Jimmy Greaves and George Mills, before the war.) By now, though, all was not well at Stamford Bridge, and Dave Sexton became increasingly withdrawn. An appallingly sloppy performance on Boxing Day, when Chelsea squandered a two-goal lead to lose 2–4 to West Ham, was a sign of things to come. One or two of the players looked in a dream – it was the start of a long, unhappy period in Chelsea's history.

II The Agony

Suddenly everyone was talking about Chelsea's new stand, while the barracked team, so recently kings of Stamford Bridge, must have yearned to join the company of those yellow-helmeted building labourers watching from a growing jungle of scaffolding while the team fumbled on the pitch. While some of the players had grown their hair longer, it seemed their ability to play the game of football was sadly impaired, and, to make matters worse, there was high-speed friction in the dressing-room. It was back to the early 1930s again, with petty jealousies and player power snipping and sniping at the daily training programme.

When Sexton dropped Bonetti, Hudson, Osgood and Baldwin for the 1974 New Year's Day match, hostile dragoons assembled at the gates of Stamford Bridge. A rift was coming, and did so in dramatic fashion. Osgood and Hudson, the former a veritable court jester and debonair

Alan Hudson, a prince of dribblers . . .

. . . pictured here displaying a West Coast look as he signs an autograph for a young Chelsea fan, Judith Albrow, who also took the picture.

Peter Osgood . . . with Afro.

dandy, and the latter a sleek-haired admirer of social life in darkened disco cellars, failed to take part in a training session at Mitcham before a third round FA Cup tie against Queen's Park Rangers, and the axe came down. Chelsea suspended both forthwith and put them on the transfer list.

A straightforward personality clash between Sexton, the introvert, and the two outgoing buccaneers, Ossie and Hudson, had instigated the poison. Eventually Osgood was transferred to Southampton (where he later won a second FA Cup winner's medal) for £275,000, and Hudson to Stoke City for £240,000 and the bonus of the odd England cap. On reflection, their departure from Chelsea marked a premature decline for a pair who should have gone on to capitalize on their gifted talents for far longer than they did. As for Chelsea, their form in later months was deplorable, despite the recall of Cooke from Crystal Palace for a mere £17,000.

What also worried the Chelsea board was the sudden decline of support after years of heavy patronage. Only 8,171 turned up to watch a re-arranged match against Burnley – Chelsea's then lowest League attend-ance since the war. Suddenly, Chelsea were struggling in the relegation zone, a situation they once regularly experienced; but now a novelty, and a dangerous one. There was this editorial in the Chelsea programme early in 1974, which was hardly cheering: 'There comes a time in everyone's life – at work, within families, in sport – when there is a clash of personalities, and it is evident that for some time such a situation has existed at Stamford Bridge between manager and one or two players. Occasional rifts are part of the internal life of every club. When they have happened at Chelsea, every effort has always been made to breach such rifts, as indeed was done in this case. But since Peter Osgood and Alan Hudson were insistent that the situation could not be improved, the board felt that they had no alternative but to make them available for transfer. In so doing – and obviously we part with players of their talent with great reluctance – we would like to thank them for their services to Chelsea and wish them success in the future....'

Sexton needed to find another team to fill the streamlined new stand ready for the launching of the 1974–75 season. In July 1975, Sexton bought David Hay from Glasgow Celtic for £225,000, Chelsea's last major signing of the decade. Hay, an elegant midfield player and defender, had done well for Scotland in the recent World Cup Finals in West Germany,

The great Gordon Banks shakes hands with his old England companion Peter Bonetti after Stoke City had gained a surprise 2-1 victory over Chelsea in the League Cup Final, March 1972.

Brian Mears in front of Chelsea's streamlined new stand, which was opened in 1974. The venture was to lead to severe financial complications.

Ron Harris receives his illuminated address from Chairman Brian Mears at his testimonial – April 1980.

and he was considered the man to give Chelsea a boost in the new season ahead.

When Brian Mears, who had every excuse to be a harassed chairman at the time, unfolded the new stand to the Press, there was a mood of optimism about the proceedings. The stand looked impressive, although some of the more fastidious journalists present doubted their future ability to cope with Thames-side wind-breaks in the exposed reporting box, while seating at the top of the stand hardly helped those who suffered from vertigo. But the colossal price of the new metal object, and the dainty fitness of the players working out with Sexton on the pitch, mellowed such pessimism.

Then came some harsh truths. Chelsea, instead of beating the newly promoted rustic Carlisle United at Stamford Bridge on the first day of the season, promptly lost, and supporters excited by the prospect of a new era began to have doubts again. Building bills at Chelsea had soared, that giant construction of steel and concrete was already bleeding one of the country's great clubs to death, although the signs were not widely apparent at the time. As the team dawdled, despite the influx of gifted young players like Ray Wilkins, Gary Locke, Ian Britton and John Sparrow, manager Sexton became the first victim of Chelsea panic, sacked in October 1974. Sexton, Chelsea's most successful manager, was by no means finished, however, continuing in management at Queen's Park Rangers, Manchester United, where he was shamefully sacked in 1981 through pressure from the fans, and Coventry City.

Man management at Chelsea lacked stability from then on, right through to the start of the 1980s. After a spell as caretaker, Ron Suart was appointed team manager, with Eddie McCreadie flung into the deep end as player-coach with a view to taking over, which eventually he did in April 1975.

But Chelsea were already destined for relegation by then – an amazing slide, considering how highly they were regarded four years before. It took McCreadie two years to bring Chelsea back to the First Division with a side motivated by Ray Wilkins. Some of the old faces were still around – Bonetti, the 'Cat', recovering his place from John Phillips, and inscribing a new record in the Chelsea book with over six hundred appearances; Ron Harris, still master of the 'ordained' destruction job, and another amazingly long server. And younger faces like Graham Wilkins, Ray's brother, at left-back; Micky Droy, at centre-back, a veritable, hard jaw-

boned colossus; Britton, Sparrow, Locke, Kenny Swain, and leading
scorer, Tommy Langley, scorer of an elegant goal from the blind side
against Wolves at Molyneux to confirm promotion in 1977. And Charlie
Cooke still wove miracles in mid-field, although soon to find a new
soccer career in the United States.

Promotion had been vital for a club desperately enmeshed by financial
pressures. There were rumours that Barclays Bank had been threatening
to call in their massive loan for the two-million-pound stand. By May
1976, Chelsea's debts had soared to £3.4 million, and Martin Spencer, a
financial wizard, had been called in to deal with the danger. There was
more trouble on the managerial side to come. Only two months after
Chelsea were promoted to the First Division in 1977, McCreadie, wearer
of those ominous dark glasses in the manager's dug-out, had gone. He
resigned, unable to agree personal terms of a new contract ... or, alter-
natively, so it was said, the club unable to accede to his demands for a
ten-year contract.

Meanwhile, Spencer burnt the midnight oil – the club was in a crisis
state, the worst in their history. But by bringing about a moratorium
Spencer bought essential time with the creditors, enabling Chelsea to
survive the very real threat of extinction. But in doing so, he did not
always see eye to eye with team managers, who needed cash for new
players. But while managers left the club with frightening rapidity,
Spencer remained, subsequently appointed a director and chief executive.
By the start of the 1981–82 season, Spencer's hard work had not been in
vain ... the debt was down to £1.3 million.

But Chelsea supporters were in rebellion. The departure of McCreadie,
ultimately into American football, was considered a disaster, and loyal
supporters like Henry Turner, a jovial extrovert from the Rag Trade,
blasted the Chelsea establishment in the club bar: 'Sheer rubbish, old
chap. They ought to move Fulham in here.' The appointment of former
youth coach Ken Shellito, who had been with the club for twenty-two
years since joining as a junior, was a managerial failure. Shellito went
before eighteen months were out, and Chelsea were on their way to the
Second Division again. The surprise appointment as his successor of
Danny Blanchflower, the gregarious former Northern Ireland and Spurs
captain, now a journalist, came too late. Chelsea went down.

Blanchflower, whose insatiable love of football did not obscure his
reservations about the state of the modern game, would happily chat

Peter Bonetti, Chelsea's longest-serving goalkeeper, caught giving the ball a more than suspicious inspection, through the lens of the *Observer*'s award-winning sporting photographer Eamonn McCabe.

about tactics and theories into the early hours of the morning on away trips . . . but somehow what he had to say to the Chelsea team did not always tick. There was a lack of response, a lack of teamwork, the old bug continued to harass the team. Duncan McKenzie, considered a brilliant ball artist and striker, arrived from Everton, failed to deliver, and left. Blanchflower's most intriguing signing was Petar Borota, a Yugoslav international keeper. Borota, a talented artist with paints in his spare time, wanted to show the Stamford Bridge crowd that Bonetti, the retired 'Cat', had nothing on the Yugoslav 'Puma'. He had everything except consistency – he was brilliant, awful, courageous, clownish. Borota showed he loved the theatrical, dashing out to kick clear, or sauntering upfield to make a handy pass to a colleague. His appreciation of crosses worried his bosses; he dropped some, and lost goals; sometimes he headed the ball away; but he remained a firm favourite of the Stamford Bridge crowd, always lovers of an oddball.

Blanchflower appointed Geoff Hurst as his coach, the England 1966 World Cup hero who scored a hat-trick against West Germany – or, as photographic evidence suggested, didn't. It was still an unhappy time at the Bridge, and after Ray Wilkins was transferred to Dave Sexton's Manchester United for Chelsea's record outgoing transfer fee of £750,000, Blanchflower bowed out and Hurst took over. At that time, the manager exchange rate at Chelsea was so high that Brian Mears might have been entitled to patrol the Fulham Road in search of the nearest stranger to offer the job to.

Mears had another problem at Chelsea – escalating hooliganism. A national and social problem begun in the 1960s had not abated, but rather worsened. The old bullet-headed pioneers of violence had retired, but the bovver boys remained, to wreck trains and intimidate innocents on the terraces and in surrounding streets. Chelsea's record had become one of the worst, and the fencing around the pitch was not always enough to prevent violence. Chelsea's 'Shed', although populated by many true young lovers of the game and passive followers of the Blues, harboured the hard core. And Mears had regularly to dissociate the club from the mischievous deeds of a small minority of the fans.

After Hurst was appointed in October 1979, he made Bobby Gould his assistant. At first, the combination looked like bringing Chelsea up again. A bold bid for promotion was made that season, but Chelsea had to be content with fourth place – hardly the stuff to cheer the creditors.

Ray Wilkins.

Steve Wicks.

Clive Walker, foraging up field against Notts County, 1980.

The next season proved calamitous after Chelsea had made a positive start. An effervescent 6-0 win in October against Newcastle United, with Chelsea employing three wingers in Peter Rhoades-Brown, Clive Walker, and Phil Driver, proved deceptive. By the half-way stage, Chelsea held a five-point lead over the fourth club, but then the team simply evaporated. They scored in only three of the season's last twenty-two League matches, and failed to earn a goal at all in the final nine, ending up in twelfth place, the lowest final position in their history. Again the guillotine was sharpened as the fans protested. In April, Hurst and Gould were sacked, each with eighteen months of his contract unfulfilled. Hurst later dropped a proposed High Court action against the club for wrongful dismissal, after Chelsea agreed to pay him 'substantial compensation'.

More trouble was to come behind the scenes after that barren season. In appointing former Middlesbrough (and previously Wrexham) manager John Neal, a forty-eight-year-old north-easterner from Seaham Harbour, Co. Durham, as their sixth manager in seven years since Dave Sexton left, Chelsea at last abandoned a policy of going for first-time managers in favour of someone with thorough managerial experience.

Neal's appointment cost him a few warm digs in the ribs from his manager friends when he visited a FA coaching course a few weeks later. Malcolm Allison winked: 'I can see you now, John,' said the former Manchester City bear, 'wandering along the Kings Road, jangling with jewellery, and clicking your fingers in time to the music on your walk-about head-phones.' Neal soon showed his players, reporting back for training, that the new season was not going to be a walk-about – he planned to 'murder' his players in training. And in return, some of the discontented stayed on after all.

But there had been boardroom changes. Neal was still settling into his office at the Bridge in the silence of a late spring morning when Brian Mears looked in. 'I've got some bad news for you,' he said. Neal, with a wry smile, replied with a streak of north-eastern humour: 'This must be a record – I've only been here two days.' Mears added: 'I've resigned.' So the chairman had packed it in, a good man, unfairly abused by the mob, and now free to enjoy his seat as vice-president, with Lord Chelsea stepping into the chair. Certain things would not be the same any more, like those hen tea parties given after matches by the chairman's dynamic brunette wife, June, or even his own vague attempts

Chelsea's unpredictable Yugoslav goalkeeper Petar Borota displaying his
powers of ball control against Goddard of QPR – Loftus Road 1979.

to suppress a frown after another failure by his beloved club to find the rigging.

Danny Blanchflower provided the perfect send-off for Mears in his *Sunday Express* column – and one that conveniently closes this chapter about one of the most lovable, exasperating, inconsistent, comic, sensational clubs in the history of football. Wrote Blanchflower: 'Brian Mears grew up at Stamford Bridge as a boy, looking forward to school holidays when he could watch his royal blues run out from under the old grandstand. He was the prince of the Bridge, and then one day he inherited the kingdom. There were good times before the bad. The night that Chelsea won the Cup in 1970 and then, a year later, the night they won the Cup-Winners' Cup.

'They had to do something about the old stand. It would fall down if they did not. So they spent a lot of time planning a new one to match their winning desires and ambitions. They spent too long thinking about it. And the stand they planned was too grand. Rising prices and the growing freedom of footballers crippled the club. It was a bridge of troubled waters when I joined them. I knew they were looking for a miracle, and I knew I did not have the miracle they needed. But maybe I could help them help themselves. It was worth a try.

'The times I spent at Stamford Bridge were not easy ones. Yet I enjoyed them and I learned a lot about Chelsea and Brian Mears. Brian was always a decent and amiable man with me. He could still laugh when pressures mounted and he was devoted to Chelsea, a very friendly place, but not for a football manager when they were after his blood. Some said Brian was not a good chairman because he listened to too many people and could not make a decision. I do not know about that. Chelsea were trapped in a financial crisis when I was there, and there were not too many decisions you could make. . . .'

So the great-nephew of the founder, Henry Augustus (Gus) Mears, and the son of the popular Joe, who saw the club through hard times after the Second World War, stepped aside. A new era at the Bridge was about to begin.

11

Conquerors of Liverpool
...but no Promotion

In retrospect, Stamford Bridge's new era had hardly begun before it was eclipsed by another. By the end of the 1981–82 season, Chelsea were under the control of a new chairman, property man Kenneth Bates, who had bought the club literally out of the blue in April. The Bates take-over subsequently led to a boardroom exodus, in which the bearded millionaire replaced Lord Chelsea as chairman, and five directors departed, including that ardent Chelsea fan from Richmond, Sir Richard Attenborough.

Thus the boardroom upheavals, which had been so much a part of Chelsea's recent history, returned to prominence as Chelsea's promotion assault towards the First Division withered away again. By the time cricketers donned spring pads, and Ron Greenwood announced his England World Cup squad for Spain, Stamford Bridge had become resigned to another season of Second Division football. For this biographer, the compiling of a final chapter proved a headache as Chelsea, under their new manager, John Neal, and assistant manager Ian McNeill, swooped back and forth between performances ranging from the very exciting to the banal. But, then, wasn't this Chelsea all over, fooling us all to distraction with their unpredictability?

Famous victories over Liverpool, the European champions, and subsequent English champions, in the fifth round of the FA Cup, and Southampton, in the third round of the Football League Cup, preceded the club's failure to win promotion – manager Neal's prime aim when he took over in the summer of 1981. Chelsea never capitalized on a fair start when they took thirteen points from seven games. Excuses there were, later; the loss through injury of that trojan defender, Micky Droy, hardly helped matters – but too many goals were missed, too many silly goals let in. The failure of so many squad players to sustain a reasonable level of consistency would in the end prove too severe a handicap for any promotion assault. So Chelsea had to sit back and watch talented sides like Luton Town and Elton John's Watford soar up to the seniors.

It was certainly a blow to Neal – an astute, knowledgeable manager, but handicapped with restrictions on buying new talent. When Chelsea lost their zest towards the end of the season after the defeat by Spurs in the FA Cup sixth round, attendances at Stamford Bridge, which required a break-even figure of 20,000 to nurse Chelsea's financial debts, drifted down to a record low. Depressing, but times nationally were hardly happy either. The season included one of the coldest winters on record, which turned the Bridge into a Siberian iced lake; a national rail strike; and finally the most destructive happening of all, the Falklands crisis involving Britain and Argentina, which escalated brutally after the Junta's invasion of the Islands. Chelsea Football Club had experienced wars before, and here was the club again, trying to extricate themselves from their own playing and financial problems, as Prime Minister Thatcher, an SW3 resident, tackled her own.

For Chelsea, the problems were freewheeling. The invigorating Cup run, and a brief, lingering hope of Chelsea reaching another Wembley final, provided a major, happy distraction. Otherwise, there had been serious problems involving the hooligan faction, who call themselves Chelsea supporters, while their behaviour is more suggestive of the farmyard. A full-scale riot at Derby County's Baseball Ground in late November, in which this section on their violent path inflicted £2,500 of damage, ended with a temporary ban by the Football Association on Chelsea supporters travelling to away matches. So the loyal majority suffered at the hands of the warmongering minority.

Lord Chelsea, the chairman, said at the time that it was impossible to keep Chelsea fans going to away matches without a ticket. And he was proved right – the fans kept travelling, and after a large crowd of troublemakers acted menacingly at Vicarage Road, Watford, early in the new year, and were let into the ground to prevent trouble outside, the FA eventually lifted the ban. Stamford Bridge also had its crowd troubles

Geoff Hurst.

Danny Blanchflower.

John Neal.

MATCH | MAGAZINE 50p
Chelsea

THIS WAS TO HAVE BEEN A COLOURFUL, COMMEMORATIVE FRONT COVER FOR TODAY'S GAME.
HOWEVER, DUE TO THE PROBLEMS CAUSED BY A SMALL LUNATIC FRINGE WHO PERSIST IN CAUSING TROUBLE FOR THE CLUB, WE HAVE BEEN FORCED TO ALTER THE DESIGN IN ORDER TO MAKE THE FOLLOWING STATEMENT:
IF YOU ARE HERE, MASQUERADING AS A FOOTBALL SUPPORTER, BUT YOUR SOLE PURPOSE IS TO CAUSE TROUBLE, THEN YOU ARE *NOT* WELCOME. YOUR BEHAVIOUR AS WITNESSED IN THE PAST, WILL NO LONGER BE TOLERATED. NOT ONLY WILL WE ENSURE THAT YOU ARE EJECTED FROM THE GROUND AND BANNED FOR LIFE FROM STAMFORD BRIDGE, BUT ALSO CHELSEA FOOTBALL CLUB WILL NOT HESITATE TO BRING A PRIVATE PROSECUTION AND CIVIL CLAIM FOR DAMAGES AGAINST YOU.

FA CUP ROUND SIX
TODAY'S MATCH SPONSORED BY BOVIS
Tottenham Hotspur
SATURDAY, 6th MARCH, 1982
KICK-OFF 3.00 p.m.

For Chelsea's quarter-final match against Spurs the club printed this unique notice in the match programme.

when 41,412 fans watched the Liverpool cup-tie ... with the result that the club printed a memorable warning to troublemakers on the cover of their sixth-round programme. With the problem a national one, and as old as time, it would take another long sociological study to fathom it. One had met a number of fans of the more unruly Chelsea element, and found their ideas not only dangerous but fragmented with hate. The racial overtones of their conversation, in pubs, on trains and in stadiums, have been nursed by their own domestic frustrations and lack of opportunities. The club, unluckily, has become a base to voice these frustrations to the detriment of fun and entertainment.

Mihir Bose, an Indian soccer writer from the *Sunday Times*, was one victim last season of Chelsea fan aggression, discovered minding his own business on a train to St Pancras from Nottingham. He no longer travels on trains on match days. To the twelve bullies involved, this book is not dedicated.

Added to Chelsea's hooligan problems were rumours that the club would have to sell Stamford Bridge to solve the continuing financial problems. One had to admire the sterling way in which manager Neal kept at his task of running a football team. The headlines could hardly have helped his morale, but with North-Eastern spirit he kept doggedly on. At times, he did have positive reason to produce that benign smile of his in face of the Press. The first major one came in October when Chelsea went down to the Dell to take on Southampton, and Kevin Keegan, who were doing well among the leaders of the First Division. Petar Borota had been injured in the ribs in a previous match, and although a pain-killing injection would probably have done the trick, Neal decided not to risk the erratic Borota. Instead he chose the inexperienced Steve Francis, a seventeen-year-old apprentice. It was a début that revealed mature qualities sufficient to banish Borota, the Yugoslav international, to reserve team football.

Chelsea came away with a 1-1 draw at the Dell, Mike Fillery equalizing Keegan's first-half goal, which Chelsea had disputed as handball. Francis was delighted by his debut, telling Peter Blackman of the *Evening Standard*: 'I had a few shakes at the start. Kevin certainly handled the ball on the line later when he scored.'

Southampton came to the Bridge for the replay and lost out after extra time by 2-1, Clive Walker earning praise from his manager for his renewed appetite for the game. Walker scored Chelsea's first goal with a

Clive Walker scores Chelsea's first goal against QPR, Boxing Day 1981, when
Chelsea won 2-0.

The Sunday Telegraph's sports photographer Phil Sheldon vividly captures the heading power of Chelsea's Micky Droy, defending in the same match.

header, Fillery heading the winning goal with a resounding thump in extra time.

Progress in the League was not sustained, however. After the euphoria of victory over First Division opposition, Chelsea went to Rotherham and crashed out by 6-0. And in the fourth round of the League Cup, Wigan Athletic from the Fourth Division proved too waspish for the Blues, winning by 4-2. Not every match was a failure, however. Chelsea travelled to the Valley and won 4-3 - one of the goals, a ferociously struck 35-yard drive by John Bumstead, likened by *Daily Telegraph* correspondent Paul Ward-Smith to the goal scored by Aarie Haan of Holland against Italy in the 1978 World Cup.

By Christmas, things were looking up in the promotion stakes - and Chelsea did themselves proud, after absorbing all the pressure going on Queen's Park Rangers' Omniturf pitch, by scoring two late winning goals. Droy was a veritable colossus.

Interlocked with the appalling winter weather were the opening brushes between senior sides striving for Wembley. Chelsea hardly looked worthwhile contenders during their delayed 0-0 draw against Hull City at Stamford Bridge. Francis, six foot, twelve stone, the Basildon apprentice, who was still required to sweep out the dressing-room after matches, and clean his colleagues' boots, kept his side in the competition with two good stops. 'Steve has a very promising future, but working as an apprentice and helping out are all part of a young lad's football education,' his manager said approvingly. For Francis, the rewards would be a lucrative new contract with his club, and a place in the England youth squad. A worthy successor to Peter 'The Cat' Bonetti had been discovered.

Chelsea won the replay against Hull with goals from Alan Mayes and Bumstead, but it took two replays to dispose of Wrexham in the fourth round, both cast iron encounters. The first match at the Bridge was drawn 0-0, and Mayes saved the Chelsea bacon six minutes from the end of the first replay. In the second replay in Wales, Droy, with a backheader, and Mayes put Chelsea into the fifth round. Mother Fortune released a real plum in the draw - a meeting at Stamford Bridge with Liverpool.

On paper, Chelsea's chances against the European Champions looked as flimsy as a discarded stocking. Bob Paisley's reshaped team were in superb form, and firm favourites to win the FA Cup. Neal quietly assessed his tactics - at least, he knew his team would give everything. To come was

February, 1982. Lee celebrates with Rhoades-Brown, the scorer of the first goal in Chelsea's 2–0 victory over Liverpool in the fifth round of the FA Cup. Photographed by Eamonn McCabe, 1982 Sports Photographer of the Year.

a famous, unexpected victory – one of the finest in Chelsea's history, won by two clear goals.

The framework of victory was laid after only eight minutes by Peter Rhoades-Brown, the forward with the Etonian-sounding name from Hampton, Middlesex. It was a moment so thrilling that the scorer would watch it over and over again in action replays, scarcely believing his eyes. After McDermott lost the ball in midfield in competition with Lee, Rhoades-Brown went racing off on the stodgy pitch at Lee's instigation, pausing slightly to drive the ball away from Grobbelaar into the net. Pandemonium reigned – it was quite like the old days at Stamford Bridge.

After this rude awakening, Liverpool understandably began to click, with Dalglish, Rush and McDermott threatening the Chelsea goal. Rush and McDermott almost claimed goals with shots that hit the upright and crossbar, but Fillery and Droy inspired the Second Division side as the clock ticked on with Paisley's team still one down. In the second half Liverpool replaced McDermott with Johnston, but by now their challenge had lost its bite. Neal, always vulnerable to probing runs by Walker and Rhoades-Brown, finally came a cropper by providing a free shot for Colin Lee to score Chelsea's winning goal with six minutes remaining. Walker, perhaps a fraction off-side, centred across goal and after Grobbelaar palmed the ball away, Neal's knee provided the exit to Liverpool's Cup ambitions.

The final whistle sent young Chelsea rejoicing en masse on the pitch like a whirl of locusts. A happy day for the club, especially as the away ban on Chelsea supporters had been lifted a day before. There was a mood of 'We can't believe it' along the Fulham Road as one of the heroes, Rhoades-Brown, slipped quietly away to see his father in hospital. The headlines revealed all next day – ETON BALL GAME! – FIGHTING FARE – AMAZING – TWO STEPS TO HEAVEN – PETER'S THE HERO. ... The Sunday writers manfully wrote their Cup obituaries of Bob Paisley's team, while the beaten manager remained dignified in defeat, praising Chelsea resolve and purpose on the day.

Brian Glanville (*Sunday Times*) remembered other times when Chelsea had dumbfounded the bookies: 'Chelsea, astonishingly, have done it again; but then, it has always been dangerous to write them off in cup-ties when they appear to be the underdogs. So, just as they did four years ago, they have knocked out mighty Liverpool by a margin of two goals.

Steve Francis took Borota's place as Chelsea's first team goalkeeper in 1981. The 17-year-old Dagenham boy showed tremendous promise in his first senior season. In this photograph by Phil Sheldon, he seems to be suspended on an air cushion.

Of these, the first was a thrilling and unexpected thrust, the last a strange Liverpudlian catastrophe. . . .'

Hugh McIlvanney (*Observer*) praised Chelsea's teamwork: 'Behind Droy, Francis, a remarkable precocious goalkeeper at seventeen, played with marvellous authority, drawing further attention to the inconsistencies of Grobbelaar in the other goal. From the midfield Fillery aimed the ball around aggressively, and the attacks were given a real edge in the first half by Colin Lee's appreciation of space and the speed of Rhoades-Brown. . . .' Frank McGhee in Monday's *Daily Mirror* praised Paisley's sportsmanship: 'He was the first to congratulate Chelsea on their astonishing, gutsy FA Cup win and then steadfastly, wittily, rejected all the excuses offered to him at his post mortem conference. . . .'

Neal, overjoyed, was also overawed by the convincing thoroughness of the performance: 'To be honest, I didn't quite expect our lads to respond in the manner they did. I think it was a marvellous experience for everyone present to witness the way in which we won the match, which earned us another tie of the round' (against Spurs, the FA Cup holders at Stamford Bridge).

Thus Chelsea, sitting pretty on an upset described by David Lacey of the *Guardian* as 'the biggest surprise of the season', prepared for the visit of a team of rich talent, a Spurs team which could call on Glenn Hoddle, Ray Clemence and Osvaldo Ardiles. It was a formidable sixth round challenge – and one for which Chelsea found themselves handicapped even before they started. Colin Lee, so forceful against Liverpool, was unable to play because of suspension after a momentary loss of cool in a League match against Cardiff. Meanwhile an injury to Droy also ruled him out of the game – and his absence was to prove costly.

Even so, Chelsea gave Spurs a fright when Fillery scored an exceptional goal two minutes before half-time. Colin Malam set the scene in the *Sunday Telegraph:* 'Taking the free kick some twenty-five yards out, Fillery hit the ball with such force and controlled its trajectory so well that Clemence was left groping as the missile flew into the net high to his right. It was the perfect time to take the lead (Walker had been pushed by Hughton to earn the free kick) and everyone assumed that Chelsea had gained a significant advantage. Everyone, that is, except Spurs, who decided the moment had come to impose themselves on the match. . . .'

Chelsea crumbled, Spurs scoring three second-half goals in the first eighteen minutes. Malam reported: 'Three minutes into the second half, a free kick just outside the Chelsea penalty area was teed up by Ardiles for Hoddle, and Francis was unable to hold the midfield player's wicked low shot as he dived to his left ... Archibald was on hand to put the ball away....' Hoddle added a second for Spurs with a momentous 25-yard shot, and the crafty Hazard plugged a third. Easy, easy.... Mayes' second goal for Chelsea was hardly enough to inspire another giant-killing. So Spurs were safely through – on their way, eventually, to their second successive FA Cup triumph.

The glorious run was over – no need, now, to produce a list of old Chelsea warriors like Ossie and Dave Webb to attend spring celebrations along Wembley way. Had Chelsea drawn Crystal Palace in the quarter-finals and Leicester in the semis, they might have done the trick. But that is might have been. The blow had been struck, as Ken Jones, *Sunday Mirror* writer and my former Army PT instructor, pointed out, by Hoddle's goal – 'It had a concussive effect on Chelsea's youngsters. They could forget about Wembley.'

An anti-climax set in at Stamford Bridge, but at least chairman Bates's take-over provided optimism that blue shirts and round balls would go on flourishing at the Bridge. The old brigade hoped so, the young brigade hoped so.... Bates, as Colin Gibson recorded in the *Daily Telegraph*, 'ended doubts surrounding the club's future and gave it financial security lacking since the golden days of the early 1970s.'

Bates, a millionaire from Beaconsfield, who used to be a director of Wigan Athletic, bought the club in April after eleven weeks of negotiations, but did not inherit the $£1\frac{1}{2}$ million debts. The deal, worth a substantial sum, means that the holding company SB Properties will continue to own the ground and will mortgage it to pay the debts. Bates will lease the stadium from the holding company for seven-year periods.

Optimism flowered. Bates made an expansive gesture in handing a bottle of champagne to each Luton player at the Bridge, after they had been promoted. Perhaps he was hoping for a similar personal party at the Bridge next season.

'I know', he said, 'that Chelsea is one of the most exciting clubs in London, a sleeping giant, a stately home run down. With care, patience and enthusiasm, we can be back in the First Division – where we belong.'

Play it again, Pensioner Percy.

Chelsea fans await their club's famous victory against Liverpool.

Back endpapers: the 1981 Chelsea squad. Back row (*left to right*): Michael Nutton, Colin Lee, Colin Pates, Micky Droy, Paul Williams, Phil Driver, Paul Ward. Middle row: Norman Medhurst (*head trainer*), Ron Suart (*chief scout*), Peter Rhoades-Brown, Timmy Elmes, Gary Chivers, Bob Iles, Petar Borota, Michael Fillery, Gary Locke, Mick Leach (*youth team coach*), Eddie Franklin (*physiotherapist*). Front row: Ian McNeill (*assistant manager*), Graham Wilkins, Kevin Hales, Clive Walker, Dennis Rofe, Colin Viljoen, Ian Britton, John Bumstead, Alan Mayes, John Neal (*manager*).